T0160165

Transatlantic Transformations: Equipping NATO for the 21st Century

Daniel S. Hamilton, Editor

Hamilton, Daniel S., ed. *Transatlantic Transformations: Equipping NATO for the 21st Century*. Washington, D.C.: Center for Transatlantic Relations, 2004

© Center for Transatlantic Relations, Johns Hopkins University 2004

Center for Transatlantic Relations
The Paul H. Nitze School of Advaned International Studies
The Johns Hopkins University
1717 Massachusetts Avenue, N.W. Suite 525
Washington, D.C. 20036
Tel. (202) 663-5880
Fax (202) 663-5879
Email: transatlantic@jhu.edu
http://transatlantic.sais-jhu.edu

Cover photos courtesy of NATO; German Ministry of Defense.

Table of Contents

Acknowledgements

On behalf of the Center for Transatlantic Relations at the Paul H. Nitze School of Advanced International Studies I would like to thank the Bundeswehr Center for Analyses and Studies, and the POBB Program of the Ministry of Foreign Affairs of the Government of the Netherlands, for their encouragement and support of this project. The Center for Transatlantic Relations sponsored study group sessions of the authors and other experts in Washington and in Europe, and we are grateful to our partners and our hosts for those occasions. Particular thanks go to Chantal de Jonge Oudraat, Esther Brimmer, Katrien Maes, Jeanette Murphy, Ralph Thiele and Tjarck Roessler for their help throughout the project. Each author writes in his personal capacity, the views expressed are those of the authors and not their institutions.

Daniel S. Hamilton

About the Center
for Transatlantic Relations

The Center for Transatlantic Relations, located at the Paul H. Nitze School of Advanced International Studies, near Dupont Circle in Washington, DC, engages international scholars and students directly with government officials, journalists, business executives, and other opinion leaders from both sides of the Atlantic on issues facing Europe and North America. Center activities include research projects and policy study groups; media programs and web-based activities; seminars and lectures.

The Center also coordinates the activities of the EU Center Washington DC—the American Consortium on EU Studies (ACES)—which has been recognized by the European Commission as one of a select number of Centers for European Union Studies in the United States. The EU Center is a partnership among five national capital area universities—American University, George Mason University, George Washington University, Georgetown University, and The Johns Hopkins University—established to improve understanding of the EU and U.S.-EU relations.

Transatlantic Transformations: Equipping NATO for the 21st Century

Chapter 1

What is Transformation and What Does It Mean for NATO?

Daniel S. Hamilton

This volume examines the implications of U.S. defense transformation for the NATO Alliance, particularly how and whether America's allies and partners can or should close a looming "transformation gap" with the United States. While there has been no effort to force consensus among the authors in this volume, a basic theme does connect the various contributions: if Alliance transformation is to be successful, it must include but also go beyond the purely military dimension. NATO must transform its scope and strategic rationale, its capabilities, its partnerships, its very ways of doing business.

What is "Transformation?"

"Transformation" is a term favored by the Bush Administration to describe a wholesale reorganization of U.S. defense policy and priorities in response to what the Administration perceives to be the threats of the 21st century. George W. Bush first used the term transformation in a 1999 speech at the Citadel in South Carolina to describe how he would change the U.S. military if he were elected president.[1] Since that time, the term has been woven into most Presidential speeches on national security issues, and has been a key driver of U.S. defense policies and budgetary priorities.

Over the past few years, however, the term has lost much of its original focus. Officials and pundits have been using the word "transformation" to describe everything from reorganization of the federal government to reorientation of foreign policy priorities. Commentators often equate "transformation" simply with "change." The result has been confusion about the exact nature of the Bush

---

[1] "A Period of Consequences," Speech delivered by George W. Bush at The Citadel, September 23, 1999, http://citadel.edu/pao/addresses/pres_bush.html.

Administration's transformation agenda, and what it may mean for America's allies.[2]

In the United States, the most specific use of the term "transformation" has been in relation to military forces. In its simplest interpretation, transformation is understood as the application of information technologies to the conduct of warfare. But it also means a good deal more. One of our authors, Hans Binnendijk, describes transformation as the process of creating and harnessing a revolution in military affairs.[3] It includes new capabilities harnessed to new doctrine and new approaches to organization, training, business practice and even culture.

Understood in this way, U.S. military transformation did not begin with the Bush Administration. The current revolution in military affairs may in fact be traced to ongoing changes in technology, in operational utilization of that technology, in associated organizational changes, and in broad new approaches to conflict based on the changing strategic environment accompanying the end of the Cold War.[4]

This ongoing revolution in military affairs is "transforming" the entire way the U.S. military organizes and trains for warfare, even how it thinks about it. U.S. military services are making dramatic strides in changing the way they fight. They are shifting from force-oriented to capability-oriented approaches to military planning; from attrition-based force on force warfare to effects-based operations; from terrain-based to time-based capabilities; and from segmented land, sea and air services to shared awareness and coordination across

---

[2] The Administration's National Security Strategy, for example, uses the term transformation interchangeably to describe federal government reorganization, responses to terrorism, military modernization, and even changes in U.S. policies toward India. *National Security Strategy of the United States of America 2002*, www.whitehouse.gov/nsc/nss.html See also the discussion on "Building Capabilities—Realizing Military Transformation," at the 2002 Dwight D. Eisenhower Security Conference, September 27, 2002, available at www.eisenhowerseries.com

[3] See Hans Binnendijk, "Introduction," in Hans Binnendijk, ed., *Transforming America's Military* (Washington, DC: National Defense University, 2002). For a description of transformation by the Director of the Office of Force Transformation in the Office of the Secretary of Defense, see VADM (ret.) Arthur K. Cebrowski, "What is Transformation?" http://www.afei.org/transformation/pdf/WHAT_IS_TRANSFORMATION.pdf

[4] A key marker in the process was the Pentagon's *Joint Vision 2010*, produced in the mid 1990's, with its focus on massing fire rather than massing forces. U.S. Joint Chiefs of Staff, *Joint Vision 2010* (Washington, DC: U.S. Department of Defense, 1996). See also U.S. Joint Chiefs of Staff, *Joint Vision 2020* (Washington, D.C.: U.S. Department of Defense, 2000).

all military services, or what is termed the "joint" force. They are focusing more on asymmetric threats. They are focusing on smart weapons, space-based systems, and C4I (command, control, communications, computers and intelligence) capabilities that can be used to synchronize and "leverage" the capabilities of the entire force, and technologies and practices that can save manpower and increase lethality and survivability.[5]

The U.S. Navy's new doctrine of network-centric warfare, the U.S. Army's shift toward light, flexible and quickly deployable units that can be integrated into information networks, the U.S. Air Force's development of the global strike task force, the U.S. Marine Corps shift from intermediate staging bases to direct projection of naval combat power to onshore targets, and the creation of the U.S. Joint Forces Command (USJFCOM) to experiment with different doctrines and to drive transformation throughout the military are only a few examples of the changes underway. These innovations are fueled by large increases in spending and a $400 billion defense budget.

What Does Transformation Mean for NATO?

The U.S. transformation effort has profound yet uncertain implications for America's allies. Washington is pushing NATO to base its own evolution on U.S. "transformation" efforts. Admiral Edmund Giambastiani, who both heads the U.S. Joint Forces Command and serves as NATO's supreme allied commander for transformation, describes transformation as "a strategic opportunity and a pivotal moment for the Alliance. The prize is improved interoperability, fundamentally joint, network-centric, distributed forces capable of rapid decision superiority and massed effects across the battle space, critical to continuing Alliance relevance."[6] Former SACLANT Admiral

---

[5] Former SACEUR Joseph Ralston describes these processes in "Keeping NATO's Military Edge Intact in the 21st Century," Presentation to the NATO/GMFUS Brussels Conference, October 3, 2002, available at http://www.nato.int/docu/speech/2002/s021003d.htm. For further discussion of effects-based operations, see Paul K. Davis, *Effects-Based Operations (EBO): A Grand Challenge for the Analytic Community* (Santa Monica, CA: RAND, 2002)

[6] Admiral E.P. Giambastiani, Supreme Allied Commander Transformation, "Transformation is a continuing process, not a destination," http://www.act.nato.int/transformation/transformation.html.

Forbes underscores this view: "A transformational process akin to that which has been taking place in the United States is essential to modernize the Alliance's capabilities and ensure that they stay consistent with U.S. military thinking and development."[7]

Others are skeptical. They question whether America's European allies share the Bush Administration's enthusiasm for "transformation," and doubt whether they are prepared to do—and spend—what may be required by such sweeping revisions of defense policies and priorities. Yves Boyer argues in this volume that in the wake of the Iraq war and other tensions between the Bush Administration and key European allies, efforts at "Alliance transformation" may no longer coincide with the diverging strategic perspectives of the U.S. and many of its European allies.

Even senior Alliance officials who support "transformation" as a process for the Alliance resist the notion that U.S. efforts can simply be transplanted onto NATO. "Can the American Transformation process be exported as is to NATO?" asks General Harald Kujat, Chairman of NATO's Military Committee. "The answer to that is a resounding "no" and I will tell you why…When dealing with Transformation, NATO must consider a very specific challenge that does not encumber U.S. Transformers: Multinationality of Sovereign States."[8]

Others downplay the need for Europeans even to keep pace with U.S. efforts. The U.S. and its allies have struggled for half a century with gaps in capabilities, questions of interoperability, and debates about burden-sharing. These debates have not stopped NATO nations from working together in robust, complex and difficult missions from Bosnia to Baghdad and from Kosovo to Kabul. Moreover, the argument goes, European strengths lie in greater development of "civilian power"—pre- and post-conflict management, peacekeeping, mediation, monitoring, and foreign assistance. Instead of trying to match the U.S., a global superpower, Europeans should stick to what they do best. These are old debates, and the critics ask, "What's new?"

---

[7] Interview with Admiral Ian Forbes, *NATO Review*, Summer 2003, http://www.nato.int/docu/review/2003/issue2/english/interview.html

[8] General Harald Kujat, "The Transformation of NATO's Military Forces and Its Link with U.S. Transformation," http://www.nato.int/ims/2003/s030121e.htm.

What's new is that the U.S. may now simply be pulling away, due to a combination of strategic reorientation, accelerating leads in military technology, sheer spending on defense, and transformational concepts. What's new is not a capability gap but a looming "transformation gap"—a potential breach in strategic orientation, spending priorities, conceptual and operational planning and training. If the U.S. comes to believe that NATO is not relevant to its most serious security challenges, then U.S. officials will treat NATO as the 10th planet beyond Pluto, interesting to behold yet quite distant from earthly concerns. This view is already espoused within senior echelons of the current Administration.

The authors in this volume approach the issue of NATO transformation from different perspectives. They offer different—and sometimes conflicting—prescriptions. As a whole, however, their argument is straightforward. If Alliance transformation is to be successful it must include but also go beyond the purely military dimension. NATO must transform its scope and strategic rationale, its capabilities, its partnerships, its very ways of doing business.

Transformation in Scope and Strategic Rationale

In the following chapter former NATO Secretary General George Robertson explains how NATO has been engaged in an ambitious defense transformation agenda since the end of the Cold War. At the 1999 Washington Summit, NATO leaders acknowledged terrorism and the proliferation of weapons of mass destruction to be key challenges for the Alliance, and they acted on that challenge in September 2001, when they invoked for the first time the Article 5 mutual defense clause of the North Atlantic Treaty following al-Qaeda attacks on New York and Washington, D.C. They did so again by sending forces to Afghanistan to fight al-Qaeda and the Taliban, and to support and eventually command the International Security Assistance Force.

These events ended the perennial debate in the strategic community whether NATO could or should go "out-of-area." Whether this view is fully shared among parliamentarians and the public in Europe and North America, however, is still questionable.

At the Prague Summit in November 2002 the Alliance moved further. Allies agreed that NATO forces must be able to "deter, disrupt and defend" against terrorists, and that they should do so wherever the interests of NATO nations demand it. NATO's command structure was reformed to include a new Allied Command Transformation to drive European transformation. Agreement was reached on the creation of a NATO Response Force (NRF) to engage quickly and effectively in high-end operations. By bringing together the best forces from both sides of the Atlantic, the NRF has the potential to serve as a catalyst for the transformation of all Allied forces. Allies also agreed to a "Prague Capabilities Commitment" to make major improvements in such key areas of modern operations as strategic transport, interoperability, and precision-guided munitions.

These are significant achievements. But transatlantic bickering over Iraq demonstrates that it will be hard for NATO to use the military forces at its disposal effectively—with or without the NRF—unless there is a greater agreement among NATO's nations on the nature of future threats. There are varying views among allied nations, and individual efforts are not yet incorporated into a coherent Alliance strategy anchored by support by opinion leaders and the broader public on both shores of the Atlantic.

Will current geopolitical differences destroy NATO's abilities to provide the military basis for future coalition operations? Boyer argues that the main issue is not whether NATO can evolve into a more effective organization, but whether Alliance leaders can find common ground in their views of the world.

Hans Binnendijk and Richard Kugler argue forcefully in this volume that NATO's defense transformation agenda, no matter how vigorous, will lack a compelling strategic purpose and in the end prove ineffective unless it is accompanied by the second part of a dual-track strategy that gives equal weight to NATO's political transformation and strategic realignment. The fact that most European allies did not participate meaningfully in the Afghanistan war demonstrated NATO's need for defense transformation, but the war in Iraq highlighted NATO's need for strategic realignment by opening fissures that could cripple the Alliance's ability to act coherently outside Europe.

Binnendijk and Kugler set forth the specific elements of a second track strategy for strategic realignment. It would include a new "Harmel Report," a strategic vision of threats, goals, priorities, and standards for using military force, particularly in out of area engagements; give the NATO decision-making process greater flexibility and responsiveness; organize NATO forces for stabilization and reconstruction capabilities; and create a new "Partnership for Cooperation" (PFC) to help foster cooperative military ties between NATO and partner countries in the Greater Middle East.

To their already full agenda I would add another element: aligning Alliance doctrine, capabilities and civil-military emergency planning with national strategies to defend the "transatlantic homeland." In past years NATO reforms have focused on projecting force and coping with threats beyond the NATO area. But NATO's nations—and their partners—must be equally prepared to prevent, deter and, if necessary, cope with the consequences of WMD attacks on their societies—from any source. Territorial defense in the Cold War sense of protecting sea-lanes from Soviet submarines or guarding the Fulda Gap from Soviet tanks must give way to a new common conception of territorial protection against WMD attacks from any source. Europe cannot assume that it will not be a target of future terrorist attacks. Al-Qaeda has attacked NATO ally Turkey. Al-Qaeda cells have tried to launch attacks in other parts of Europe as well. If Alliance nations fail to defend their societies from a major attack using weapons of mass destruction, the Alliance will have failed in its most fundamental task. It will be marginalized and the security of Europe and North America will be further diminished.[9]

Developing common or complementary approaches to what Americans call homeland security and what Europeans call societal preparedness and protection is a major priority for the transatlantic community. In most countries these issues are primarily civilian, national and local priorities. But NATO has a role to play, particularly in civil-military planning capabilities and in consideration of missile defense. NATO's civilian disaster response efforts are still largely geared to natural disasters rather than intentional attacks, and remain

---

[9] See Daniel S. Hamilton, "Renewing Transatlantic Partnership: Why and How," Testimony to the House Committee on International Relations, European Sub-committee, June 11, 2003; Daniel S. Hamilton, "Our Transatlantic Homeland," http://www.raeson.dk/indexenglish.htm; Terrence K. Kelly, "Transformation and Homeland Security: Dual Challenges for the US Army," *Parameters*, Summer 2003; Jonathan Stevenson, "How Europe and America Defend Themselves," *Foreign Affairs*, March/April 2003

very low priority. It is time to ramp up these efforts to address intentional WMD attacks on NATO territory, and to work with partners such as Russia to develop new capabilities and procedures for collaboration with civilian authorities.

In fact, the area of "transatlantic societal security" could be an attractive new mission for a revised Partnership for Peace, since after the next round of NATO enlargement the Partnership will become a strange mix of prosperous, non-aligned Western countries such as Sweden, Finland, Austria, Ireland and Switzerland, and a number of Central Asian nations. It is precisely some of these non-aligned countries, however, which have decades of experience with approaches to societal defense, and it is precisely the area of Central Asia in which forward defense and preventive efforts against WMD threats are critical. NATO's special partnerships with Russia and Ukraine could also be utilized to good effect in this area.

Harnessing Transformed Capabilities to New Military and Civil-Military Action

Effective NATO transformation will also depend on the degree to which European capabilities will be harnessed to the transformation revolution driving the U.S. military. Boyer is skeptical, not only whether European nations will do this, but whether they should. He is wary that such efforts could hook Europeans into a particular "American way of war," which should be resisted. Our other European authors are less skeptical, but Rob de Wijk and Andrew James each argue that any successful European effort to develop transformational capabilities will have to be tailored to particularly European requirements, and will have to be done via the track of deeper European integration.

Current gaps are striking. First, there are gaps in sheer spending. Although Europe's overall economic potential rivals that of the United States, European spending on military power is half that of the United States. Second, there are wide gaps in defense research and development (R&D) spending. The U.S. spends close to six times what EU nations spend on military R&D. U.S. expenditure on military R&D alone is greater than Germany's entire defense budget. Third, there are spending gaps per service member. U.S. spending per active duty service member is almost four times that of Europe 's. Fourth, there are gaps in the cost-effectiveness of spending. Although Europeans spend about half what the U.S. spends, they get less than 50% return in terms of capability, and little of it is spent on the power-projection missions of most relevance to the U.S. [10]

These disparities add up to an enormous gap in capabilities between U.S. forces and even the most modern of European NATO forces. This transatlantic divide, in turn, is exacerbated by equally wide gaps among European forces themselves. Proportionately, whatever the measure of effort, the discrepancies between European leaders and laggards are even greater than those between Europe and the United States. Rob de Wijk demonstrates these disparities very clearly. While cautioning against the assumption that "smaller" nations possess less capability than "larger" nations, he shows how NATO has essentially developed into a five-tier alliance regarding military capabilities, ranging from the full spectrum force of the U.S. to those with capabilities to project power and deploy force, those wedded to Cold War postures, primarily new members will modest capabilities, and some who have little real capability at all.

These shortfalls are difficult to manage politically. They reinforce stereotypes on both sides of the Atlantic and produce different perceptions of risk, cost and success. Europe's relatively sluggish efforts fuel American critics, who question whether U.S. allies have truly grasped the dimensions of change underway and whether they are prepared to make the decisions needed to fight alongside Americans or even to be militarily valuable partners for the United States. European allies, in turn, have been both impressed and demoralized by the sheer extent of U.S. military spending, which seems to exacerbate the challenges of interoperability and keeping pace with American technology. Cavalier or bellicose Administration rhetoric about "the myth of NATO," "old and new Europe," or "disaggrega-

---

[10] Ralston, op. cit.; James Appathurai, "Closing the capabilities gap," *NATO Review*, Autumn 2002, http://www.nato.int/docu/review/2002/issue3/english/art1.html NATO Assistant Secretary General Robert G. Bell, "The Pursuit of Enhanced Defense Capabilities," January 24, 2002. For an American perspective on transformation and NATO's capability gaps, including detailed figures on allied capabilities, see Charles L. Barry, "Coordinating with NATO," in Hans Binnendijk, ed., *Transforming America's Military*, op. cit., pp, 230-258.

tion,"[11] on the other hand, together with its demonstrated preference for ad hoc coalitions over formal alliance structures, has fueled European critics, who question whether the U.S. truly wants allies and whether American military prowess is leading the U.S. to consider war as a readily available instrument of American diplomacy.

The capabilities gap also threatens to impose a dangerous division of labor regarding global hot spots, with the U.S. primarily engaged in the "cooking "—high-risk, high-intensity military action—and most Europeans doing the "dishes"—post-conflict reconstruction and rehabilitation. While all of our authors may not agree, this author believes such a division of labor to be corrosive to Alliance unity—and overall effectiveness. It encourages American unilateralism, European insularity, and mutual resentment. It leaves Americans with the world's most difficult and dangerous missions. It leaves Europeans with little influence on U.S. military operations yet saddles them with significant political, economic and social costs and consequences of those actions. As Stephen Larrabee has noted, such arrangements are difficult to sustain politically even when there is a high degree of agreement on aims and policies, as has been the case in the Balkans since 1995. It becomes deeply corrosive when consensus doesn't prevail within the Alliance, as is the case regarding Iraq. It provides fertile ground for a new alliance of convenience between American neoconservatives and European Gaullists who together seek to make the case for strategic divorce.[12]

As Manfred Engelhardt points out, this problem has its roots in the very structure of the Alliance, in NATO's military response to the Cold War and the threat of Soviet invasion of Western Europe. Put simply, for the United States and, to a lesser extent, the United

---

[11] Under Secretary of Defense Douglas Feith is credited with "the myth of NATO" statement; Defense Secretary Donald Rumsfeld publicly classified European allies opposed to U.S. intervention in Iraq as "old Europe" and those supporting U.S. intervention as "new Europe;" and "disaggregation" refers to internal discussions within the Administration whether the U.S. should break with a half century of support for European integration and cohesion and openly favor a looser, "disaggregated" Europe.

[12] See Stephen Larrabee and Francois Heisbourg, "How global a role can and should NATO play?" *NATO Review*, Spring 2003, http://www.nato.int/docu/review/2003/issue1/english/debate.html; David Gompert and F. Stephen Larrabee, *America and Europe: A Partnership for a New Era* (Cambridge: Cambridge University Press, 1997); Daniel S. Hamilton, "Reconciling 9/11 and 11/9," in Simon Serfaty and Christina Balis, eds., *Visions of America and Europe: September 11, Iraq, and Transatlantic Relations* (Washington, D.C.: CSIS Press, 2004)

Kingdom, NATO was a power-projection mission, while for continental Europe and especially Germany it was an issue of territorial homeland defense. The commitment to defend West Germany at its eastern border, 3,500 miles from Washington, required the U.S. to deploy thousands of troops across the Atlantic and to defend the north Atlantic sea lines of communication—even while responding globally to other possible Soviet challenges.[13] The military requirement for Bonn was to defend itself, together with its allies. The notion that the Bundeswehr would have to deploy to protect and defend others was simply alien to West German defense concepts and would have aroused considerable unease among Germany's neighbors.

Since unification the Bundeswehr has been an important institutional mechanism for east and west German integration. But whether it can really make the switch to a "transformed" force is a pivotal question for Alliance transformation. Transformation favors those forces that have already been structured for power projection—i.e. the U.S., and to a lesser extent the UK, France and the Netherlands—and requires substantially more effort from those forces structured for stability operations—i.e. much of the rest of European NATO, and particularly Germany. Engelhardt provides a detailed account of the Bundeswehr's transformational journey.

Capability differences do not only reflect the past, however. They also reflect current political differences regarding military priorities. Many European governments do not perceive the same magnitude of new threats or imagine fighting the kinds of wars that are driving U.S. innovation. Therefore, adapting their military forces to ensure they could win those wars is of lesser priority. Even if expectations were more closely aligned, Europeans would be constrained by their defense budgets. As a result, the Europeans are developing fewer innovations and experiencing less change in the most advanced military capabilities.

What can European forces do to relate to U.S. transformation efforts? The Prague Summit's answer to this challenge, as noted above, was the Prague Capabilities Commitments, the creation of the

---

[13] Binnendijk and Kugler propose new U.S. force structures in Europe in this volume. For another perspective on the future of U.S. troop presence in Europe, see the testimony by Thomas Donnelly to the House Armed Services Committee, February 25, 2003.

NATO Response Force, and replacement of the old Supreme Allied Command Atlantic (SACLANT) with Allied Command Transformation (ACT). Common to both ACT and the NRF is the insight that instead of tackling the rather insurmountable task of closing the overall capability gap, NATO nations can in effect seek to bypass it by integrating European forces into training and conceptual revolutions associated with U.S. transformation.

Just because Europeans can't do everything with Americans doesn't mean they can't do anything. Transformation is not about capabilities alone, but capabilities harnessed to new ways of conducting military action. Resources and new applications of technology are important. But equally important are such issues as training, organization, doctrine and leadership development. ACT and the NRF offer opportunities for European forces to engage with North American allies in these key dimensions of transformation. Binnendijk and Kugler propose a "NATO Transformation Roadmap" to keep the Prague initiatives on track.

Engelhardt and de Wijk outline further steps being taken in Europe to address these gaps. Even though they come from different perspectives, our European authors essentially conclude that the goal must be to develop a military posture that would be co-operable with U.S. forces but not co-determinant with U.S. force posture, and would also advance the political and strategic needs of the EU. For de Wijk and James the opportunity is to pursue network *enabled* operations (a key premise of British military thinking), rather than more ambitious network *centric* operations. Only the full spectrum force of the United States, they argue, is capable of network centric operations.

Much of the focus on Europe's capabilities gap, however, ignores a second, and equally troubling, capabilities gap, this time on the part of the United States: the gap between U.S. capacity to wage war and to secure peace. This is reflected in a whopping imbalance in U.S. budget priorities: close to $400 billion is allocated for defense but only about $15 billion for civilian aspects of international crisis management. The U.S. is fundamentally reshaping its military doctrine without similarly improving its ability to prevent conflicts or to stabilize and transform post-conflict environments.

The Pentagon's transformational goal of "full spectrum dominance" oddly fails to encompass the full spectrum of security. In most post-conflict environments the most important security challenge is providing civil protection and security. This is a job for police, not unprepared soldiers or ill-trained civilians. A 2003 CSIS Commission on Post-Conflict Resolution[14] criticized current U.S. mechanisms for international crisis management as outdated and ill-suited to addressing the complex set of challenges created by failed states. As a consequence, the military gets "stuck" with a broad range of non-military challenges for which it is unprepared. Moreover, since the Pentagon has strongly resisted any systematic effort to integrate such tasks into its strategic culture, the response to such crises is often ad hoc improvisation, marked by a reluctance to commit energy and resources and framed by an excessive focus on exit strategies, even though the U.S. military seems to exit one nation-building crisis only to enter another.

This situation is further exacerbated by America's congenital Attention Deficit Disorder when it comes to foreign policy. It is striking how quickly the attention of the media, the public and the Congress shift after a conflict is over, leaving large questions about the sustainability of support for American engagement in post-conflict situations. The result: schizophrenic engagements in Haiti, Somalia, Bosnia, Kosovo, Afghanistan and Iraq.

The U.S. must equip itself with a broad-ranging set of instruments that would give it greater capacity to wage peace as well as war. America's own "capability gap" can be enhanced through deeper cooperation with its European allies, who have advanced more comprehensive concepts for crisis management that include both civilian and military means and put particular emphasis on crisis prevention.

NATO can develop as an important multilateral forum in which to organize peacekeeping and to develop common principles governing future interventions. The NATO Response Force is a welcome development in this regard. But it has not been flanked by similar efforts to improve joint or complementary U.S. and European capacities to carry out post-conflict security tasks. We are working on only one half of the puzzle.

---

[14] *Play To Win: Final Report of the Bipartisan Commission on Post-Conflict Reconstruction* (Washington, DC: Center for Strategic and International Studies, January 2003)

Binnendijk and Kugler present various ideas to advance Alliance capabilities for stabilization and reconstruction. Consideration should be given to the creation of an integrated, multinational security support component that would organize, train and equip allied and partner units—civilian and military—for a variety of post-conflict operations. These units should be designed flexibly to support operations by NATO, NATO and Partners, the UN, and the EU. The EU's "civilian" Headline Goals, for example, little noticed in the U.S., provide for new capacities in policing, the rule of law, civil administration and civil protection, to enhance European capability to field teams that can provide comprehensive and integrated security support, especially in the aftermath of conflict.

Finally, the George C. Marshall Center in Garmisch has proven to be a useful training ground for military officials from across the Partnership for Peace. The Euro-Atlantic community has no equivalent for post-conflict reconstruction and rehabilitation operations. Since the EU plays an important role in this area, consideration should be given to an international training center for post-conflict stabilization and reconstruction operations, supported jointly by NATO and EU nations and their partners.

Transformation of NATO's Partnerships

This leads to the need for NATO to transform how it works with partners. Here there are two issues. The first is the issue of "the mission determines the coalition," and the second is NATO's relationship with the EU.

Many Europeans were upset by comments by Secretary of Defense Rumsfeld and his deputy Paul Wolfowitz during the Afghanistan war that "the mission determines the coalition," implying that NATO allies no longer enjoyed pride of place in their relations with the United States. The phrase, however, is a commonplace: the mission *does* determine the coalition. NATO was the right coalition for the Cold War mission of defending the European continent and providing a security umbrella under which west European reconciliation and integration could advance. It was also the right coalition for extending security and stability to central and eastern Europe and for dealing with massive human tragedy in the Balkans. As Alliance command of the International Security Assistance Force in Afghanistan demonstrates, NATO can also be the right coalition to protect transatlantic security interests from new threats emanating from new sources— wherever they may be—*if* Alliance nations are prepared to advance together a path of serious transformation.

All of these post-Cold War initiatives, however, have been carried out by NATO in conjunction with other partners. Given the difficulty in achieving consensus on how and when to confront new threats, together with the multi-dimensional nature of such threats, most non-European operations are likely to be conducted by "coalitions of the willing and able." The benchmark for the Alliance's future relevance in this regard should thus not be whether such operations can be conducted by NATO alone, but rather by NATO as well.

The changes in the nature and sources of threats and risks means that NATO must be prepared to respond to every type of contingency. The particular role NATO might play must be flexible. "The Alliance must be prepared to engage in a variety of international responses," notes U.S. Deputy National Security Adviser Stephen Hadley, "ranging from NATO-led missions and NATO-supported missions to instances where NATO members, and perhaps even NATO itself, would be part of a broader coalition of the willing."[15]

NATO's role as a producer of interoperability remains essential if European and U.S. forces are going to be able to work together and address many of the new threats they will face in the future. The NRF can be a catalyst in this regard by improving interoperability among "first military respondents," to borrow Francois Heisbourg's phrase drawn from the language of counter-terrorism.[16]

In short, not only must NATO nations become network-centric or network-enabled, the Alliance itself must become "network-enabled" as a key player able to plug into wider networks of alliances and coalitions. George Robertson underlined this notion of networked

---

[15] Stephen Hadley, US Deputy National Security Adviser, "Challenge and Change for NATO. A US Perspective," October 3, 2002 http://www.nato.int/docu/speech/2002/s021003e.htm.

[16] See the contribution by Francois Heisbourg, op.cit

alliances at the activation ceremony for ACT. "What makes {ACT and NATO transformation] so different and distinctive," he said, "is that it's not just simply going to be about keeping the United States interoperable with the allies but it's with a much wider family and constituency than that. We see it as being a network that involves the European Union, the partner nations, possibly even Russia, to make sure that the freedom loving people of the world are on top of the capabilities that are going to be required to deal with some very new challenges in the future."[17]

Networked threats will need to be met with networked responses, in which the NATO Alliance forms perhaps the densest weave in the network. Indeed, in this new strategic context, as Heisbourg notes, NATO can play a major role in making the formation of meaningful coalitions possible.[18]

This is where the next dimension of transformation kicks in: transformation of the uneasy NATO-EU relationship into a true strategic partnership. Dual enlargement of the EU to 25 and NATO to 26 members in 2004 makes 19 countries members in both organizations. Julian Lindley-French summarizes the possibilities:

> The potential for a synergistic EU-NATO relationship is clear. The mission of the European Union's European Security and Defense Policy (ESDP) is progressively to harmonize the security concepts and cultures of European states so that they can gradually take responsibility for civil and military aspects of security at the lower to middle levels of intensity and develop a distinct doctrine for multilateral peacekeeping and peacemaking that both organizations lack. The continuing and ever more vital role of NATO is threefold: to ensure a continuum between lower and higher levels of intensity, i.e. escalation dominance; to ensure that Americans and Europeans can work together in joint pursuit of security world-wide; and to assure the core defense guarantee so that re-nationalization of security within

---

[17] George Robertson, Press conference after ACT ceremony, June 19, 2003 http://usinfo.state.gov/topical/pol/nato/03061921.htm

[18] Heisbourg, op. cit.

Europe will not destabilize Europe's political base and prevent Europe's emerging projectability. It is as simple and
straightforward as that.[19]

Initial steps have been made. A set of key NATO-EU cooperation
documents, known in the jargon as the "Berlin-Plus" package
launched during the Clinton Administration, was finalized after rather
painful and prolonged negotiations on March 17, 2003.[20] The "Berlin-
Plus" arrangements comprise four elements: assuring EU access to
NATO operational planning; making NATO capabilities and common assets available to the EU; developing NATO European command options for EU-led operations, including the European role of
NATO's Deputy Supreme Allied Commander Europe (DSACEUR);
and adapting the NATO defense planning system to allow for EU-run
operations.

These cooperative arrangements facilitated the EU's Operation
Concordia in the former Yugoslav Republic of Macedonia, a peacekeeping mission it assumed from NATO on April 1, 2003. Daily EU-
NATO operational coordination takes place in Bosnia and
Herzegovina (where NATO-led forces are deployed in SFOR and the
European Union has a police mission) and in Kosovo (where NATO-
led forces are deployed in KFOR and the European Union is responsible for economic reconstruction). The EU conducted an
"autonomous" peacekeeping operation in the Congo in the summer of
2003 and is set to take over from NATO in Bosnia in mid-2004, with
the UK as the lead nation. NATO and EU experts are working
together on the EU's European Capabilities Action Plan and NATO's
Prague Capabilities Commitments.

Tensions resumed during the raw months of the transatlantic crisis
over Iraq, however, when those European nations most opposed to
U.S. intervention in Iraq proposed the establishment of an indepen-

---

[19] Julian Lindley-French, "The ties that bind," NATO Review, Autumn 2003,
http://www.nato.int/docu/review/2003/issue3/english/art2.html

[20] The term "Berlin Plus" is a reference to the site of the 1996 meeting where NATO ministers agreed to create a European Security and Defense Identity and make Alliance assets
available for that purpose. The EU and NATO established formal relations in January
2001 but the breakthrough came in December 2002 with the adoption of the EU-NATO
Declaration on ESDP (for full text, see *NATO Press Release* (2002) 142).

dent military headquarters, with an independent planning capacity, for a new small core of EU nations committed to deeper defense integration. The Bush Administration reacted with alarm, and U.S. Ambassador to NATO Nicholas Burns labeled the effort "the greatest threat to the future of the alliance."[21]

An uneasy resolution was finally reached in December 2003: a small EU operational planning cell is being established within SHAPE to plan for "Berlin-plus" contingencies, and NATO can liaise with the EU Military Staff in Brussels, which will have additional planning capacity for EU civilian operations and civil-military missions. This bitter interlude underscored once again how difficult it is to advance real partnership between NATO and the EU, despite the hard won practical arrangements now in place. Differences over strategy and respective roles have been shelved, not solved.

At times, the almost mind-numbing detail associated with efforts at NATO-EU cooperation make it easy to reduce this issue to a policy wonk's nightmare: hopeless, but not serious. But ESDP and NATO-EU cooperation are not marginal technical issues. They are emblematic of a central debate: how—and whether—Europe and the United States can align the grand experiment of European integration with a strategic shift of the transatlantic partnership to tackle together the challenges posed by the post-Cold War, post-911 world. Unfortunately, the allies are ducking this fundamental question, preferring instead to squabble over technical details.

Those in Europe who believe that they must weaken NATO to strengthen ESDP are only likely to achieve an insecure and incapable Europe unsure of itself and its role in the world.[22] If they want Washington to support ESDP, they must produce real capabilities and assume real peacekeeping responsibilities, for instance in Bosnia. Those in the United States who believe that strengthening ESDP means weakening NATO are only likely to achieve a lonely super-

---

[21] Ian Black, "Rumsfeld Tries to Cool Row over EU Military Plan," *The Guardian*, December 2, 2003, www.guardian.co.uk/international/story/0,3604,1097703,00.html.

[22] See Lindley-French, op. cit. For a fuller discussion of the EU's efforts to build a security and defense policy, including American perspectives, see Esther Brimmer, ed., *The EU's Search For A Strategic Role: ESDP and Its Implications for Transatlantic Relations* (Washington, D.C.: Center for Transatlantic Relations, 2002)

power unable to count on the added abilities and resources of its allies when it comes to facing new threats and risks. If they want European support for U.S. initiatives, they must be willing to allow allies to develop the capacity to do so.

Failure to advance NATO-EU partnership, in turn, is likely to damage prospects for more effective defense investment, which is at the core of Europe's defense dilemma and is a fourth key aspect of Alliance transformation.

Transforming the Business of Defense

Effective Alliance transformation depends on new ways of conducting the transatlantic business of defense. As Andrew James, Jeffrey Bialos and Stuart Koehl all argue in this volume, there is presently no meaningful transatlantic cooperation in such key U.S. transformation programs as unmanned aerial vehicles (UAVs), military space, and information dominance, nor in other areas relevant to closing the capability gap or enhancing interoperability. Current transatlantic cooperative efforts are, by and large, not related to coalition force improvements in interoperability or capability, but undertaken for reasons of affordability (Joint Strike Fighter) and geopolitics (missile defense).

James, Bialos and Koehl all argue that Europe needs to take the capabilities gap seriously and ensure that it reallocates scarce defense budgets to address NATO capabilities requirements. But they also argue that the U.S. government needs to play its part in the modernization of NATO Europe's capabilities, not least by offering technology and joint programs to support European transformation and enabling this process through changes to U.S. export and technology transfer regulations.

While the authors believe that the evolution of ESDP can evolve in ways that support or strengthen NATO, coalition war fighting and open markets, they also underscore the point that mismanagement of the issue on either side of the Atlantic could accelerate moves instead toward European defense autarky and strengthen those who view European defense cooperation as a means to "counterbalance" the United States.

Bialos and Koehl argue specifically for a policy paradigm based on "supplier globalization" to promote coalition warfare, force transformation, and competition in defense markets. This approach gained currency in the 1990s as an alternative to prevailing models of defense autarky, but little progress has been made in recent years. While the authors believe that some form of transatlantic supplier integration will probably occur over time, they are rather pessimistic about its shorter-term prospects. There are opportunities. The NATO Response Force, for example, could be a catalyst for a select number of armaments and other initiatives to enhance coalition war fighting capability, and could showcase transatlantic defense industry cooperation. James discusses how transatlantic defense industrial linkages and joint ventures may provide another avenue for success.

James argues that Europe will only meet its capabilities shortfalls through a combination of strong European efforts to build "Towers of Excellence," complemented by transatlantic armaments cooperation. While James argues that a strengthened European technological and industrial base is the best way to ensure that future transatlantic armaments cooperation is balanced and in European interests, he acknowledges that constrained R&D budgets leave Europeans little choice but to acquire U.S. technologies selectively.

The Istanbul Summit presents an opportunity to advance the transatlantic armaments agenda. NATO members should reaffirm their commitment to transatlantic armaments cooperation; identify new programs in transformational technology areas that could provide the basis for future cooperation; and establish a standing conference on transatlantic armaments, export control and technology transfer issues that could provide a forum for high level dialogue between policy makers, politicians and defense industry representatives and complement the work of the Conference of National Armaments Directors (CNAD). It would be a significant advance if EU and NATO officials working in this area met in a more structured manner, and included the National Armaments Directors of EU and NATO nations.

A Transformed Alliance?

The Prague Summit opened a new chapter in NATO's transformation. But if the Alliance is to be serious about a new "transformation agenda," it has a good deal more work to do.

The Balkan Wars demonstrated NATO's need to transcend the old "out of area" debate and the Euro-Atlantic community's need to equip itself with new tools. September 11 and subsequent al-Qaeda attacks and attempts on European targets revealed the need to develop new approaches to territorial defense of the "transatlantic homeland." The Afghanistan campaign underscored the need for European defense transformation. The Iraqi war exposed the need for Alliance political transformation and strategic alignment. In each case, however, the lessons have yet to be learned fully and acted upon. On many of these issues, differences among Europeans and among Americans are as great as those between Europe and America. And yet NATO's ability to advance in each of these areas is dependent on its ability to advance in all of them. The varying perspectives in this volume reflect both the difficulties and the opportunities facing a transformed Alliance. "This ain't your Daddy's NATO"[23] anymore, but to earn the label of "truly transformed," the Alliance still has a considerable way to go.

---

[23] George Robertson, "This Ain't Your Daddy's NATO," Speech to the Center for Transatlantic Relations, Johns Hopkins SAIS, November 12, 2003 http://www.sais-jhu.edu/bin/o/s/ROBERTSON%20SPEECH.pdf

Chapter 2

Transforming NATO to Meet the Challenges of the 21st Century

George Robertson

In a sense, NATO has an image problem. During the Alliance's first forty years, cracks in Allied unity were kept to a barely visible minimum, as any fissure raised the specter of Soviet troops pouring through the Fulda Gap. As a result, the Cold War NATO generally enjoyed an image of lock-step unity, common threat assessments and shared determination to act on both sides of the Atlantic.

Since the fall of the Berlin Wall, that image has been under attack. A series of crises, from Bosnia to Kosovo to September 11th to Iraq, has triggered debate and division both within Europe and across the Atlantic. Those used to the old NATO have interpreted those debates as signs of fundamental division—which has raised, in some circles, an anachronistic sense of panic.

It is time for the Cold War thermometer to be abandoned, because it is the wrong one. In a rapidly evolving security environment, debate, discussion and change in the Alliance are not signs of impending doom—they are preconditions of NATO's continuing health and relevance.

The recent debate over Iraq was therefore not, as some would have it, NATO's death knell. It was a necessary part of the ongoing transformation of the North Atlantic Alliance, as Europe and North America come to grips with, and learn to manage together, the very new security challenges of the 21st century.

The Immediate Post-Cold War Period

In many ways, the profound debate taking place today is one that might have occurred over a decade ago, when the Cold War ended. At that time, a fundamental discussion about the future shape of the transatlantic relationship seemed to many to be inevitable. But it was put off. The character of the new security environment was by no means clear, and there was simply too much unfinished business left over from the Cold War. The transatlantic community was fully occupied with the immediate and obvious task that it still faced together—to manage the effects of the break-up of the Soviet Union, by:

- embracing the new democracies in Central and Eastern Europe, who were aspiring to their place in Europe, including its Atlantic dimension in NATO;

- entering into a consultative and cooperative relationship with a Russia that, in a sense, was both an old empire and a new state, still unsure of its European vocation; and

- addressing the conflicts in the Balkans, which were making a mockery of the idea of Europe as a zone of peace and shared values.

These were major, pressing strategic projects. They were aimed primarily at ensuring the Cold War was wound down in the best and most peaceful way possible. And as with all Cold War-era projects, it was clear that Europe and North America had still to work together to ensure their success.

Accordingly, NATO reached out to Central and Eastern Europe, through its policy of partnership and through NATO enlargement. The Alliance also worked hard, and successfully, to associate Russia to NATO and, thus, to the emerging new Europe. And NATO played a key role in pacifying the Balkans through its military engagement.

This impressive display of transatlantic unity could not, however, hide the fact that the relationship between the two sides of the Atlantic was bound to change over the longer term. As early as 1991, the Gulf War raised the question of whether NATO was still in line with post-Cold War security requirements. That conflict took place "out of area," and was fought by a "coalition of the willing," with the Alliance playing only a supporting (if critical) role. It was perhaps an early omen of NATO's future difficulties.

Also in the early 1990s, the European Union (EU) began to articulate an ambition to become a military actor in its own right, raising questions about NATO's evolution—and in the minds of the more suspicious, a challenge to NATO's future. The initial ambiguity by the United States regarding humanitarian intervention in the Balkans also signaled a profound uncertainty about how the U.S. viewed its own future role on the European continent, and indeed as a European power.

All of these changes were harbingers of the more profound debate to come. But as in most families, the issues that might cause the most upheaval were avoided by the transatlantic community until they were forced to deal with them.

The New Security Environment: Pushing NATO to the Fringes?

September 11, 2001, gave the NATO Allies no other choice but to face the future head-on. A fundamental debate about the shape and character of transatlantic security relationship could be dodged no longer. The changes in the international security environment had become too stark, too fundamental to allow a residual post-Cold War-management agenda to ensure transatlantic security, or to sustain continued transatlantic cooperation.

Both the transatlantic relationship in general and NATO in particular have had to adapt to the realization that a new, still undefined era has begun. Three changes to the security environment, in particular, stand out.

The first change is in the nature of the threats faced by the international community. Terrorism has mutated from a largely national problem combated by police and intelligence services into a challenge to international peace and security. Similarly, the proliferation of weapons of mass destruction has a new salience in an age where traditional deterrence cannot deter certain shadowy groups or individuals, and where technology can place massive destructive power in their hands. And in the age of globalization, the effects of failing states— regional instability, organized crime, terrorism and trafficking—cross borders without showing passports.

These threats can and do emerge from anywhere on earth, and with the Cold War long behind us, Europe is no longer the prism through which the U.S. will look at global security issues. Quite naturally, U.S. attention is being drawn away from the Old Continent, towards Central Asia and the Middle East. A U.S. focus beyond Europe, however, poses an implicit risk to NATO—an institution with its roots in Europe, and one that is critically dependent on U.S. leadership.

The second change is in the strategies and approaches required to defend against these new threats. After 9/11, NATO's European orientation and traditional ways of doing business suddenly seemed out of date and out of touch. The U.S.-led operation in Afghanistan also showed that ad-hoc coalitions could be formed to deal with new threats if the Alliance were not seen to be right for the job. Finally, in an age where threats can give little warning before they strike, NATO suffered from the perception in some circles that its consensual decision-making culture was too slow and cumbersome to deliver in time.

The third change concerns the military capabilities required to respond to the new threats. Rapid response, force projection and protection against weapons of mass destruction are at a premium—precisely the areas in which the United States is increasingly strong and where Europe's Cold War legacy forces are historically weak. This trend encourages those in the U.S. who advocate a more unilateralist approach, and undercuts the influence America's European and Canadian allies have to shape U.S. security policies.

In short, by September 12, 2001, a new debate about the future of the transatlantic security relationship had become inevitable. Dodging it again, as was done in the early 1990s, would not work. NATO had to face the debate head-on, even if this meant, to use John Foster Dulles' term, an "agonizing reappraisal" of the value of this venerable Alliance.

Continuities: The Enduring Transatlantic "Acquis"

Despite the fundamental need for change, NATO took on this re-examination of its mission with considerable self-confidence. Although some Americans claimed that Europe was "fading slowly in the U.S. rear view mirror," there is a transatlantic "acquis" that remains too valuable to jettison.

First, European stability remains a U.S. key strategic interest. The consolidation of Europe as an undivided, democratic and market-oriented space remains a primary objective of U.S. security policy. Only through NATO, the central legitimizing framework for U.S. power in Europe, can the U.S. play an undisputed leadership role in advancing this strategic objective, and the U.S. is not looking to surrender this role. Indeed, both NATO enlargement and the "war on terrorism" have increased the U.S. immersion in European security affairs, in particular in the field the EU calls "Justice and Home Affairs." It is therefore no surprise that there is no serious political voice in the U.S. advocating a withdrawal from Europe.

Second, Europeans and Canadians remain America's key strategic allies. This statement does not exclude a stronger U.S. focus on other regions, nor is it contradicted by the emergence of much wider "coalitions of the willing" along the model of Operation Enduring Freedom. It is true that Europe's military capabilities lag behind those of the United States, but on a global scale, Europe still ranks a firm number 2. Moreover, although the Iraq debate may sometimes have suggested otherwise, it is only in its NATO Allies that the U.S. finds a community of like-minded countries that firmly share common values, and which are pre-disposed to working with the United States. In other parts of the world, by contrast, the U.S. has to rely on bilateral and often ad-hoc relationships, sometimes with countries that do not share the same values. In the 21st century, the U.S. may be looking beyond Europe as a potential crisis area, but it will continue to have every interest in focusing on Europe as its preferred partner.

Third, the United States remains Europe's most important ally. The U.S. continues to play a unique role within the transatlantic relationship, as a vital political crisis manager as well as military "coalition-builder," both within Europe (Balkans) and beyond (Gulf). This unique U.S. role is widely accepted by the Europeans, and there is currently no serious political voice in Europe that advocates a true U.S. withdrawal from the continent. Furthermore, with Central and Eastern Europe re-joining the Atlantic community of nations through the enlargement of NATO and the EU, the number of countries arguing for strong security cooperation across the Atlantic, and between NATO and Europe, will only increase.

Marrying Continuity with Change: Three Directions for NATO's Transformation

In that context—where the changing security environment is making the old NATO increasingly obsolete, but in which transatlantic security cooperation remains essential—the logical conclusion is clear:

NATO must transform into an organization capable of defending the security, the interests and the values of its members against the threats and challenges of the 21st century.

To be effective, NATO's transformation must follow three broad currents. First, the Alliance must find a new balance between addressing its traditional, Euro-centric missions and tackling the new global threats, such as failed states, terrorism and the proliferation of weapons of mass destruction. Second, it must develop the modern military capabilities necessary to fulfill its new missions effectively. And, finally, the Alliance must learn to react quickly and flexibly to new challenges.

The Prague Summit, in November 2002, was the opportunity to deliver on all three counts. Initially billed as an "Enlargement Summit," the idea of making the admission of new members the primary focus of the meeting was dropped after "9/11." All the Allies agreed that NATO enlargement would be an historic step, consolidating Europe as a single security space from the Atlantic to the Black Sea, and from the Baltics to the Balkans. But Prague quickly became more than a stepping stone in the enlargement process. It became a milestone in NATO's transformation into a true 21st century Alliance.

NATO's New Missions and the End of the "Out-of-Area" Syndrome

First and foremost, the 21st century NATO must adopt new roles, including combating terrorism and defending against weapons of mass destruction. This is not only a recognition of the changing nature of the security environment. It is also the only way for the Alliance to remain fully engaged with the U.S. security agenda, allowing NATO to remain the key mechanism for the transatlantic community to iron out differences and establish joint positions on these and other issues. Above all, it engages NATO—the world's most effective facilitator of military coalitions—in modern operations.

Even before the Prague Summit, a NATO role in combating terrorism was being defined by two unprecedented events. The first was the invocation of Article 5 on September 12, 2001. By agreeing that a terrorist attack by a non-state actor should trigger NATO's collective self-defense commitment, the Alliance had, in effect, mandated itself to make combating terrorism an enduring NATO mission. This broadening of the meaning of collective self-defense was complemented by a second precedent: the deployment of forces from many NATO nations to Afghanistan, under the "Article 5" umbrella. This marked the *de facto* end of NATO's "out-of-area" debate, which, as one NATO Ambassador cogently put it, had collapsed with the Twin Towers.

The Summit further defined NATO's role in combating terrorism. Allies agreed to develop a military concept against terrorism and specific military capabilities to implement this new mission; on an Action Plan against terrorism which engaged NATO's Partners across Europe and into Central Asia; and on a shared commitment to act in support of the international community in combating this scourge.

NATO was quickly being redefined as a focal point for any multinational military response to terrorism. This policy re-orientation was backed up by action, with the agreement to provide Germany and the Netherlands with NATO planning and support as they took over command of the International Security Assistance Force (ISAF III) in Afghanistan. The Alliance's formal assumption of leadership of ISAF in August 2003 has established NATO firmly as an organization that can take action beyond the Euro-Atlantic area, and that is now a key actor in the international struggle against terrorism. So, too, have NATO's maritime operations in the Mediterranean to protect against terrorist attack.

A similar approach was taken with respect to the threat posed by the proliferation of weapons of mass destruction and their means of delivery. Before "9/11," NATO's efforts to counter this threat might have seemed something of an afterthought. The Prague Summit presented an entirely different picture. Various initiatives on nuclear, biological and chemical weapons defense signaled a much stronger transatlantic consensus on the need to cope with this challenge.

Technically, these initiatives, which range from enhanced detection capabilities to developing a Prototype Deployable Nuclear, Biological and Chemical (NBC) Analytical Laboratory, may seem prosaic and unspectacular. But their immediate significance is as much political as practical. They indicate a heightened awareness of a common threat, and a determination not to let the issue of weapons of mass destruction become a major transatlantic fault line. This determination was underscored further with the agreement to begin a new NATO

Missile Defense feasibility study to examine options for protecting Alliance territory, forces and population centers against the full range of missile threats.

The decisions taken up to and at Prague put NATO firmly back on track. By claiming a distinct role in combating terrorism, and by giving much more prominence to issues related to weapons of mass destruction, NATO has recalibrated its agenda both in line with the emerging new strategic environment, and with key security concerns of the allies in the 21st century.

NATO's Military Reform: Bridging the Capabilities Gap

The second major element of NATO's reform is in its overall military capabilities. For the past several years, the priority within the Alliance has been to improve the "European pillar." This process was based on the need to give Europe more military clout to look after its own backyard. Implicitly, it was also seen as a hedge against the possibility of any eventual diminishment of the U.S. role in future European crisis management scenarios.

9/11 and the Afghanistan campaign demonstrated, however, that "Europeanization" is not enough to ensure European security. Europe must also remain capable of cooperating militarily with the United States, both to allow for the most effective defense and crisis management, and also to ensure that U.S. unilateralism does not become inevitable simply for lack of military interoperability.

Even within NATO, it will be vital to avoid a two-tier Alliance, whereby, as a French observer once put it, the U.S. does the fighting and the Europeans "do the dishes." This would be politically unsustainable—both across the Atlantic as well as within the EU. Different roles in crisis management spawn differing perceptions of risk, cost and success, as the international disarray in the early response to the war in Bosnia made very clear. For an Alliance such as NATO, and indeed even within the EU, such a division of labor is slow poison, and must be avoided to the extent possible.

The Prague Summit made it clear that this risk is well understood. One of the key, but less heralded initiatives was the reform of NATO's command structure, a process which has led to the creation of a

Strategic Command focused exclusively on spurring and guiding military transformation throughout the Alliance.

Another significant decision was the adoption of the U.S. proposal to create a NATO Response Force. Not only did it signal NATO's willingness to adapt in line with the requirement for more rapid military action; it is also a catalyst to help Europeans accelerate their force transformation, a sign of a continued U.S. willingness to view the Alliance as an important military instrument, and a tool to ensure that allies share the burden of being at the "sharp end" of operations.

Progress in setting up the NRF is ahead of schedule, and the initiative has drawn offers of contributions from across the Alliance. Allies will also, however, have to look at their national decision-making processes in the context of the NRF. While NATO has demonstrated that it can take very rapid decisions (including by invoking Article 5 on September 12th 2001), some NATO nations must currently follow time-consuming procedures and processes before any deployment of forces abroad. Allies will have to ensure that NATO remains able to react quickly politically as well as militarily, in a security environment where speed can be of the essence.

Another key Summit achievement was the Prague Capabilities Commitment. Individual allies made specific political commitments to improve their capabilities in areas key to modern military operations. Once fully implemented, these commitments would quadruple the number of outsize aircraft in Europe; establish a pool of air-to-air refueling aircraft until additional new tankers will be available; ensure that most of NATO's deployable high readiness forces will have chemical, radiological, biological and nuclear defense equipment; and significantly increase the non-U.S. stocks of air-delivered precision-guided munitions.

These commitments mark a turning point in the transformation of the defense capabilities of the non-U.S. allies. If nations stick to their targets, both NATO and the EU will have taken a major step towards meeting 21st century requirements.

The urgency to make these improvements is only growing. Despite the hundreds of billions of dollars or Euros they spend on defense, allies are finding it increasingly difficult to come up with forces useable for modern operations—forces that are deployable over long distances, sustainable for long periods of time, and equipped to prevail in their missions.

Without those useable forces, the international community will have increasing difficulty meeting its current commitments, or taking on new missions in key parts of the world. Reprioritizing current spending, and finding any necessary new spending, must therefore not only be a priority on paper—it must be accomplished. NATO is helping that to happen.

NATO's Internal Reform: Towards a More Modern Organization

The third area of Alliance reform concerns the organization itself. NATO's working methods must reflect the requirements imposed by the new strategic environment. Although the Alliance will soon have 26 members, the organization's procedures and practices have remained largely unchanged from those developed in the early 1950s, for an Alliance of twelve. Even if American accusations that the Kosovo campaign was "war by committee" were overwrought, the need for change is still clear. As NATO is enlarging both its membership and its mandate, its working methods cannot be left unaffected. In a nutshell, NATO needs to be less bureaucratic, and more flexible.

Almost unnoticed by the broader public, a strong start has been made in this direction. Heads of State and Government agreed to reduce the numbers of NATO committees (currently 467) by 30 percent, which has now been achieved. More decisions will be pushed towards subordinate committees, leaving the North Atlantic Council room to discuss strategic issues. The procedures for Ministerial meetings continue to be streamlined as well, sacrificing formality in order to gain time for more substantive exchanges. Over time, these changes should lead to a different working culture within the Alliance.

But more changes may be still to come. Some analysts foresee arrangements whereby troop contributing nations "run" the operation, and decide on the targeting, while the North Atlantic Council confines itself to providing overall strategic guidance.

This model, which resembles the EU's "committee of contributors," may be seen by some as an assault on the cherished rule of consensus.

But a shift to "majority voting" in NATO remains clearly out of the question. The requirement for consensus not only generates pressure to seek compromise, it also provides countries with the "emergency brake" of a veto—an option that reassures, in particular, smaller countries that they will not be steamrolled by the bigger Allies.

In a similar vein, the idea of NATO acting on occasion as a "toolbox," i.e. as a pool from which to provide coalitions of the willing with specific capabilities, is here to stay. Indeed, NATO's support of the EU in crisis management is an illustration of how well this can work— because an EU drawing on NATO assets is precisely a "coalition of the willing" drawing on the "NATO toolbox." The challenge for NATO is to reconcile its occasional role as a "toolbox" with the continuing need for political cohesion.

Despite the quality and quantity of NATO "tools" potentially on loan, however, it is vital for NATO's long-term political health for the Alliance to continue also to lead operations under a NATO flag. This, too, seems inevitable, because NATO is uniquely capable of carrying out peace-support operations.

Literally no other organization can generate and command large numbers of multinational forces, and sustain them over long periods of time in difficult and dangerous operations far away from home. That is why the Alliance was asked to lead, and then to expand, ISAF. It is why there is pressure in many circles for NATO to take a more visible role in Iraq—and why some are already calling for NATO to contribute to the Middle East Peace Process. It is therefore essential that the Alliance puts the political and decision-making structures in place to allow it achieve its full and unique potential as a contributor to international peace and security.

Conclusion: Unfinished Business, but . . .

NATO's role in the immediate aftermath of "911" was hampered by three interrelated dilemmas. First, there was no pre-forged consensus on how to tackle the new threats with which we were suddenly faced. Second, the U.S. felt that its Allies simply did not possess enough useful capabilities to warrant going through NATO in order to round them up. And, finally, some in Washington saw NATO as an organization whose decision-making structures didn't allow for the kind of rapid and flexible response required to face modern threats in a timely way.

Today, NATO is demonstrating that it has learned these lessons. Allies have set out an emerging transatlantic consensus on how to tackle the new threats; they have launched a process that should result in more relevant capabilities across the Alliance; and they have initiated a wide-ranging reform of NATO's working methods. In a very short time, the organization has shown that a venerable old dog can indeed learn new tricks.

Institutional fixes today cannot be expected to solve all the challenges NATO will face in future. Structural dilemmas, such as the U.S.-Europe power imbalance, can only be mitigated. Differing approaches to multilateralism and the use of force can be expected to persist beyond current administrations. And as the transatlantic community looks to take on a broader range of threats, in new parts of the world, discussion and debate will be both inevitable and frequent.

But the progress achieved until now is still a major step in the right direction. It sends a clear signal that, irrespective of disagreements on individual issues, working together remains the preferred option for both sides of the Atlantic. It ensures that, as NATO transforms, it will remain the organization best placed to square the circle of multilateralism and effectiveness, thereby continuing to engage both the US and Europe. And it illustrates a fundamental new reality for NATO: that in the 21st century, transformation is not an event—it is a process that will, and must continue.

Chapter 3

The Next Phase of Transformation: A New Dual-Track Strategy for NATO

Hans Binnendijk and Richard L. Kugler

Most U.S. and European leaders want to heal the rift over Iraq by restoring NATO unity and effectiveness. But how can this worthy goal be accomplished? This urgent question requires a credible answer. Some observers argue that because the United States and Europe cannot agree on security policies outside Europe, they should limit their cooperation to such soft-power issues as trade, foreign aid, and combating HIV/AIDS. While common action on soft-power issues is useful, this strategy would leave NATO—the transatlantic community's premier military alliance—with no serious role to play in the ongoing struggle against terrorism, tyrants, WMD proliferation, and radicalism in the Islamic world. Something better is needed: a constructive security strategy for NATO that also employs hard power in sensible ways, and that both Americans and Europeans will agree upon.

Need for a New Dual-Track Strategy

We believe that such a strategy can be crafted if the United States and Europe recall how they solved similar serious problems during the Cold War. On earlier occasions, the Alliance successfully coped with an assertive American military agenda that troubled many European countries for political reasons by creating dual-track strategies that combined military modernization with new political endeavors. The first case arose in the mid-1960s, when the Alliance used the "Harmel Report" to mate deterrence and defense with détente. The second case occurred in the early 1980s, when NATO agreed to deploy Pershing II and Ground Launched Cruise Missiles (GLCM) on European soil while also pursuing nuclear arms control negotiations with the Soviet Union. After the Cold War ended, NATO successfully pursued a third dual-track strategy by engaging Russia diplomatically while enlarging into Eastern Europe.

A new type of dual-track strategy should be pursued today. NATO already has crafted the first half of this strategy: a visionary defense transformation agenda for enhancing military preparedness. Adopted at the Prague Summit of 2002, this agenda aims at fielding a new NATO Response Force (NRF) and other measures to prepare for new missions outside Europe. This forward looking defense agenda must now be pursued vigorously by promptly fielding the NRF, creating a NATO transformation roadmap, and designing a new U.S. military presence in Europe. As an urgent priority, NATO now needs to craft the second part of this dual-track strategy: an accompanying political transformation agenda for strategic realignment. The goal of this political agenda should be to achieve NATO consensus behind fresh, well-construed policies and decision processes for applying power in the Middle East and other regions to deal with emerging threats and strengthen relationships with friendly countries. Such an agenda of political transformation should include four measures that, along with military transformation, would produce a major strategic realignment of NATO:

- Writing a new Harmel Report that would help lay out a common strategic vision of threats, goals, priorities, and standards for using military force and other instruments in the Middle East.

- Reforming the NATO decision-making process to create greater flexibility and responsiveness in performing missions outside Europe in peace, crisis, and war.

- Finding ways for NATO and the Europeans to play larger roles in post-war situations where stabilization and reconstruction operations must be launched.

- Creating a new "Partnership for Cooperation" (PFC) to help foster cooperative military ties between NATO and friendly Middle Eastern militaries.

This new dual-track strategy of defense transformation for military preparedness and political transformation for strategic realignment can be adopted at the NATO summit in Istanbul in 2004. Prompt and vigorous implementation is vital, so collaboration among leading NATO powers is essential. The United States and Britain must work constructively with Germany and France, and vice-versa. The times are too dangerous to permit internal quarrels that leave the Alliance divided and adrift. If NATO is to be salvaged, the United States and Europe must want to do so. Nothing in this dual-track strategy implies that the United States and its close friends should cede the option to act outside NATO when the situation merits. Yet, both the United States and Europe will benefit if NATO can be employed consistently as a preferred instrument of choice. The new dual-track strategy is meant to make this practice possible.

Why Save NATO?

To experienced hands, the proposal that NATO pursue transformation will sound familiar. NATO has been undergoing transformation for at least a decade; Europeans began using this term long before it became popular in the U.S. military. But the NATO transformation of the early 1990s was different from that of today. Then, NATO was trying to shift from being a Cold War defense alliance toward one helping to create a Europe that was stable, whole, and free. NATO was filled with optimism and hopeful visions of a bright future for itself.

Today, transformation involves a quite different type of strategic realignment: preparing NATO to project power and purpose not on the European continent, but into the Greater Middle East and other distant areas. The environment also is different. NATO is filled with misgivings about its future as it tries to recover from a badly damaging debate over Iraq that shook its foundations.

In today's troubled setting, the idea of NATO crafting a bold political-military transformation for strategic realignment runs counter to the instincts of those who are content to see NATO lose relevance or disintegrate. Those Americans who have given up on NATO judge that the United States should act unilaterally, with only Britain and a few "cherry-picked" European allies by its side. Similarly, some Europeans see NATO as an impediment to casting off American domination and becoming independent on the world stage.

Critics on both sides of the Atlantic are right about one thing: letting NATO wither would be easier than keeping it alive and healthy. Why, then, should NATO be saved? The perfunctory answer is that an effective NATO will enable both the United States and Europe to preserve security within and beyond Europe. This truism, however, has been cited so often by NATO advocates that it has become worn and unpersuasive. A more effective way to set out what is at stake is to ask the question, "What would the world be like without NATO?"

Some observers claim that the choice is not between transforming NATO and losing it. They argue that NATO can cling to the status quo while doing little of consequence outside Europe, apart from providing a launch-pad for U.S. forces and preparing a few allies to participate in ad-hoc coalitions led by the United States. This mistaken judgment, however, is a prescription for NATO to slip into irrelevance. The United States and Europe would lose interest in NATO and would not be able to prevent its demise. A big organization without purpose eventually loses its legitimacy and will to live. After that, a slow death is inevitable.

The collapse of the Atlantic Alliance might not bother those in the media and the general public who see little value in NATO. It might please those Europeans who view the United States as an arrogant superpower. It might also please those Americans who dismiss Europe as a decadent civilization. But when the dust settles and realization grows that the world's oldest, most successful democratic alliance has been lost, a different reaction might settle in. The widespread response might not be applause, but instead anger at the short-sighted governments on both sides of the Atlantic that allowed this travesty to occur. Such governments might not stay in office for long. Even if they endured, their reputations for wise stewardship would suffer a grievous blow. Nobody would emerge a winner in the court of public opinion or the verdict of history.

Loss of NATO would damage not only the reputations of ruling governments, but also the enduring interests of the United States and Europe. A first casualty would be the war on terrorism. Although the main event has been the invasion of Afghanistan, this war is mostly being fought in the twilight, behind the scenes, and with many instruments other than military force. Tracking down small, dispersed terrorist cells across the globe requires extensive multilateral collaboration in many areas—diplomacy, intelligence sharing, law enforcement and extraditions, disruption of terrorist finances, homeland security, training and aid to foreign governments, and strikes by special forces. Moreover, the conquest of Afghanistan is now requiring peacekeeping, stabilization, and reconstruction efforts aimed at preventing the Taliban from regaining power. Today NATO is providing this multilateral collaboration or creating a framework for it to occur. If NATO vanishes, much of this cooperation would be lost, and terrorists would be given a new lease on life.

The damaging effects of NATO collapse would extend far beyond the war on terrorism into the strategic realm of traditional security affairs. For the United States, loss of NATO would be a more serious setback than advocates of unilateralism realize. At a minimum, the United States would lose influence over Europe's evolution and would face even greater anti-Americanism. In other regions, the United States might not have its wings clipped to the degree envisioned by some Europeans—a global superpower has many other friends—but it would suffer from the loss of political legitimacy that European and NATO support often gives to its endeavors in the Middle East and elsewhere. Although France, Germany, and a few others criticized the U.S. and British invasion of Iraq, fully 75 per cent of current and prospective NATO members gave vocal political support to it. Such strong support would be less likely in a world without NATO. Militarily, the United States would lose valuable infrastructure in Europe that is helpful in projecting power to distant regions. The United States also would be damaged in crises and wars that require allied force contributions. In theory, the United States could still draw upon friendly European countries to create ad hoc coalitions of the willing. But if NATO no longer exists, fewer countries may be willing to join U.S.-led coalitions. Also important, their military forces might be less able to work closely with U.S. forces because NATO no longer would provide them the necessary interoperability.

The biggest loser would not be the United States, but, Europe. NATO collapse would result in a major U.S. political and military withdrawal from the continent. The United States might retain a foothold through bilateral ties with Britain and other countries, but it no longer would play a multilateral leadership role. Along with this withdrawal would come removal of the many valuable strategic roles that the United States plays behind the scene. The United States continues to provide extended nuclear deterrence coverage over virtually all of Europe, a still-vital protection in this era of nuclear powers and proliferation. As shown in the Kosovo war, U.S. conventional forces provide about three-quarters of NATO military power-projection assets for crises and wars on Europe's periphery. These nuclear and conventional contributions, moreover, enable Europe to defend itself with annual defense budgets that are $100-150 billion smaller than otherwise would be the case. In effect, the United States is helping fund the European Union, because these savings equal the EU budget.

Perhaps the Europeans could fund a big defense buildup to compensate for loss of American military guarantees, but the price could be quite high, because a European buildup absent NATO would be costlier than a buildup under its auspices; NATO offers many economies of scale and opportunities to avoid redundancy through integrated planning. In addition, a European military buildup would be controversial. How would Europe erect an umbrella of nuclear deterrence? How would it prepare for crisis operations on its periphery? What would be the European reaction if Germany were compelled to build nuclear forces and a large, mobile military?

A European military buildup, however, seems unlikely. Is there any reason to believe that European parliaments would surmount their current anti-military attitudes to fund bigger defense budgets? Their reaction might be to slash budgets further on the premise that the collapse of NATO made defense strength less necessary and that Europe could avoid war through diplomacy. As a result, Europe might withdraw into a disengaged foreign policy. Even if bigger budgets were forthcoming, European militaries no longer would enjoy U.S. help in developing new-era doctrines, structures, and technologies. In the military transformation arena, they would be left on the outside looking in. Without U.S. contributions, they could be hard-pressed to muster the wherewithal to deploy missile defenses to shield Europe from WMD attacks. Developing serious forces for power-projection outside Europe also would be difficult, without American help in such critical areas as C4ISR, strategic lift, and logistic support. Overall, the collapse of NATO could leave Europe more vulnerable to threats across the spectrum from terrorism to WMD proliferation and less able to exert influence in the regions that produce these threats.

In addition to these adverse military consequences, American political contributions to European unity, peace, and prosperity would decline precipitously. For the past fifty years, America's constant presence has assured small European countries that they will not be dominated by powerful neighbors. It also has helped guarantee that the continent will not slide back into the competitive geopolitical dynamics that produced two world wars in the 20th Century. The U.S. presence helped Germany find a welcome role in an integrating Europe and permitted leadership by the so-called "Quad" (the United States, Britain, Germany, and France) in a manner that gained the support of other NATO members. Recently, the United States has been a leading advocate of NATO enlargement and European unification. In the absence of NATO, the European Union itself might be weakened, especially if the United States decided to selectively seek allies among EU members. Nor would the EU's influence and positive impact on world affairs be likely to increase. Indeed, the opposite could be the case.

A NATO that can project power and purpose outside Europe will greatly enhance the odds of preserving world peace while advancing democratic values. The simple reality is that the United States cannot handle the global problems of the contemporary era alone, and neither can Europe. Together, however, they can succeed. This is a main reason for keeping NATO alive and healthy, and for transforming it in the ways needed to perform new missions. The challenge facing the Atlantic Alliance is to pursue these goals in an effective manner that both the United States and Europe will support.

Carrying Out the NATO Defense Transformation Agenda—Next Steps

Pursuit of these goals is the main reason for adopting a new dual-track strategy aimed at defense transformation and strategic realignment. Fortunately, a strong foundation for the military component of this strategy already exists. The Prague defense agenda consisted mainly of three measures: 1) A new NATO Response Force (NRF) to be fielded by 2006; 2) A Prague Capability Commitment (PCC) to replace the stalled Defense Capability Initiative (DCI); and 3) A streamlined integrated military command plus a new Allied Command Transformation (ACT) to guide European military transformation. While the NRF was showcased at Prague, all three initiatives are important. As experience shows, agreeing to these measures is only the first step in a long process. What comes now is the tedious, time-consuming process of pursuing them to completion while making appropriate adjustments. In today's climate, success cannot be taken for granted. The situation calls for NATO political and military leaders to pay sustained attention to these measures to ensure that they unfold as planned. The Prague Summit agenda now needs to be modified in ways that will sharpen its focus and take into account new issues. A revised NATO defense transformation agenda should include the following three elements:

- Vigorous efforts to field the NRF promptly and in ways that overcome hurdles along the way.

- Preparation of a NATO Transformation Roadmap that, along with the PCC, will help provide focus and direction and encourage speedy progress toward transformation.

- Design of a new American military presence in Europe that supports NATO defense transformation and can work closely with the NRF in preparing for expeditionary warfare.

Strategic Motivations for Defense Transformation

The Prague agenda was the product of four developments: 1) the frustrations of the 1990s, when European forces made little progress toward remedying core deficiencies in power-projection; 2) growing perceptions of a widening transatlantic gap in new-era military capabilities; 3) the disappointments of the war in Afghanistan, when the United States declined offers of European help because most allied forces lacked the necessary capabilities; and 4) the acceleration of U.S. defense transformation in ways that open the door for European forces to acquire capabilities for expeditionary warfare.

The 1990s began with NATO sitting on the sidelines during the Persian Gulf War, but with Britain, France, and other countries contributing to the U.S.-led coalition. The victorious Desert Storm campaign ended with widespread recognition that European and NATO forces needed to improve in many areas to contribute more effectively to future conflicts. Declining defense budgets and withering public support, however, sent European improvement efforts into a prolonged stall. When the Kosovo war was waged in 1999, the United States contributed 75 per cent of NATO forces. In that airpower-dominated campaign, shortfalls in European forces were exposed in such areas as C4ISR, smart munitions, defense suppression, and all-weather/day-night assets.

In response, the Washington Summit of 1999 produced a new NATO strategic concept and a Defense Capability Initiative (DCI) aimed at strengthening European capabilities in multiple areas. Several countries, including Britain and France, announced long-range plans to upgrade their forces, but little progress was made. During 1999-

2001, knowledgeable observers fretted about a growing transatlantic gap in military capabilities for new-era warfare. While the United States had long been better than Europe at rapidly deploying forces, it was now pulling ahead in capabilities for waging war once forces arrive at the scene. Indeed, the U.S. military was creating a new form of network-centric warfare anchored in precision fires, fast maneuver, and close integration of air-ground fires. The aim was to replace the old emphasis on massed forces and separate operations by components with integrated joint operations conducted by dispersed, high-tech forces. Most European militaries were not embracing this new form of warfare. Indeed, they were moving toward a growing emphasis on peacekeeping, thus creating a widening gap not only in capabilities and budgets, but in strategic missions and burden-sharing as well.

The invasion of Afghanistan starkly confirmed NATO's need for military transformation. After NATO invoked Article 5 to wage the new war against terrorism, many European governments wanted to participate in Afghanistan. But except for Britain, the U.S. military turned aside these offers with the explanation that European militaries lacked the precision-strike assets for this new form of warfare. Only European SOF forces proved useful in the battles. After the major fighting ended, European forces performed peacekeeping. Later, NATO acquired a formal role in this mission, but this development only reinforced the growing impression that, while NATO might be helpful in cleaning up the mess afterward, it is not an instrument for serious war-fighting.

The U.S. defense transformation effort, accelerated shortly after the Bush Administration took power, opened the door to NATO defense revival for unintended reasons. The original purpose was to prepare U.S. forces for the Information Age by equipping them with advanced information networks, new weapons platforms, ever-smarter munitions, and exotic, futuristic technologies. To fund this effort at enhancing force quality, a big increase in the American defense budget was authorized. Initially it seemed that accelerating American military transformation would leave Europeans in the dust and thereby further magnify an already-big gap in transatlantic capabilities. But closer inspection showed that the Europeans did not need to mimic U.S. forces in new technologies and structures. Instead, they merely needed to develop the capacity to "plug and play" into the "system of systems" (integrated information grids) being created by U.S. forces. Moreover, many core operational concepts of transformation could be applied to European forces: e.g., the emphasis on joint expeditionary warfare, networked forces, littoral missions, close integration of air and ground fires, high-speed maneuvers, and simultaneous operations with dispersed forces.

Thus, although the Europeans were unlikely to match high-tech U.S. forces soon, they could embark upon their own form of transformation aimed at facilitating interoperable, complementary operations with U.S. forces on modern battlefields. Moreover, they did not need new, expensive weapon platforms (e.g., tanks and fighter aircraft) to become better at swift power projection and lethal strike operations. Instead, they needed improvements in such areas as joint planning, C4ISR, smart munitions, combat support units, mobility, and long-distance logistics for missions in austere areas. Acquiring these assets did not promise to be cheap, but if only a modest number were needed, they were affordable for European budgets. This promised to be the case if NATO and the Europeans focused on transforming only a small portion of their forces rather than their entire posture, which exceeded the size of U.S. forces by more than 50 per cent.

Bringing the NRF to Life

The idea of fielding the NATO Response Force (NRF) responded to this imperative. This idea was suggested by Secretary of Defense Donald Rumsfeld in reflection of a proposal from the National Defense University, and it quickly took hold in NATO and European military circles. At the Prague Summit, it was adopted with widespread acclaim as the centerpiece of the new NATO plan for defense transformation. By spring, 2003, it had been equipped with a strategic concept and implementation plan by the NATO Military Committee. SACEUR General James Jones promised quick progress—fielding of initial units by fall, 2003, instead of 2004 as originally envisioned.

Why the NRF for an alliance that already has many formations for many purposes? In the eyes of its American creators, the NRF reflects an effort to plug a serious hole in NATO military posture for new missions. Before the NRF, NATO mainly relied upon the ACE Mobile Force (AMF) and the ACE Rapid Reaction Corps (ARRC) for such missions. Both of these formations suffered from flaws. Originally conceived for limited emergencies, the AMF was too small and lightly equipped for intense combat operations too focused on continental contingencies. Moreover, NATO had already reached a decision to disestablish the AMF because it seemed unsuited to most contemporary missions. By contrast, the ARRC is a huge force of 4 heavy divisions backed by 300 combat aircraft and 100 ships that is too big and ponderous for swift deployment outside Europe. What NATO needs is an expeditionary force big enough to make a difference in high-tech strike operations alongside U.S. forces, but small and agile enough to be deployed swiftly. The modest-size but potent and deployable NRF is designed to fill this need while also enabling NATO and the Europeans to focus intently on a top-priority force rather than dissipating scarce resources in other directions.

The defense concept behind the NRF is simple but breaks new conceptual ground for NATO. Prior to the NRF, SACEUR defense planning was mainly anchored in large ground formations, with air and naval forces playing supporting roles. While this concept made sense for old-style continental warfare, it makes considerably less sense for new-era expeditionary warfare, which requires heavy doses of air and naval power and relatively fewer ground forces. Accordingly, the NRF concept calls for a truly joint posture of about 21,000 military personnel. It is to be composed of a single well-armed ground brigade task force, one or two tactical fighter wings, and a naval flotilla of 8-10 combatants with aircraft, cruise missiles, and other strike assets. These forces will be designed to operate jointly in carrying out new-era operational concepts and to be highly interoperable with U.S. forces owing to plug-and-play C4ISR systems as well as similar doctrines, weapons, and smart munitions. Equally important, the NRF is to benefit from advanced training in new-era operational concepts that will not only elevate its own combat capabilities, but also help introduce such skills into other European forces, thereby helping them pursue transformation as well.

The NRF posture is to be capable of being used in multiple different ways, e.g., as a stand-alone NATO force for limited contingencies, as the spearhead of a later-arriving deployment by larger NATO forces, or as a NATO contribution to an ad hoc coalition led by U.S. forces. It would have been ideally suited for the invasions of

Afghanistan and Iraq, two very different military operations. It thus promises to greatly enhance NATO capability, flexibility, and adaptability in an era that requires such characteristics for operations across the entire spectrum of conflict. Meanwhile, it promises to be a cutting-edge leader of European force transformation by exposing NRF units to U.S. initiatives and by helping develop new NATO doctrines through training, exercises, and experiments. As the NRF learns the lessons of transformation it can transmit them to other European forces. Over time, successive cohorts of European units will pass through the NRF experience, thereby steadily enlarging the pool of forces that have directly experienced transformation for new missions. While Northern European forces will benefit, the forces of new-member East European countries and the southern region will benefit also. For example, Polish forces will learn how to operate with their European and American allies, and will thereby become better providers of security, not just consumers.

The NRF should not be merely a NATO force configured to pursue the U.S. military's way of war. Instead, it should embody a synergistic blend of American and European approaches; both sides have something to offer in creating this force and its operational doctrines. Above all, the NRF should be capable of performing a wide spectrum of operations, not merely high-tech strikes with missiles and smart munitions. If such a flexible, multifaceted force is to be fielded, the Europeans will need to take it seriously. The same applies to the United States, which likely will need to loosen export control restrictions on some technologies.

By design, the NRF will not interfere with the EU's European Rapid Reaction Force (ERRF). The missions of the NRF and ERRF are different. Whereas the NRF is intended for high-intensity combat and expeditionary strike missions, the ERRF currently is slotted primarily for peacekeeping and other Petersberg tasks. The NRF is also to be smaller than the ERRF and differently structured. Whereas the NRF will have only 21,000 personnel, the slowly evolving ERRF will have 60,000 ground troops and enough air and naval assets to bring the total to 100,000 personnel. The biggest difference is that whereas the NRF always will be assigned to NATO integrated command, the ERRF will not be committed to fulfilling NATO missions. As a result, NATO will still need the NRF even if the ERRF eventually comes to life with better capabilities than now envisioned. Because the NRF will be a small posture, its budget costs will be low, totaling $3-4 billion per year for investments. Extra spending on manpower and operations will not be needed because the forces to be assigned to the NRF already exist and therefore do not have to be freshly created. While the Europeans will have to set priorities, they possess the manpower and budgets to support both the NRF and the ERRF, and therefore do not have to choose between them. Care, however, will have to be taken to ensure that "dual-hatting" of forces does not result in conflicting assignments for crisis response. As a general rule, European units assigned to NRF duty or preparing to assume this duty should not have additional assignments elsewhere, including to the ERRF. When these forces come off NRF duty, standard practices for dual-hatting can be followed.

The NRF is to be a ready force that can deploy within a week to a month and have 30 days of sustainment in intense combat. It is to be anchored in a rotational readiness scheme. During any six-month period, a full-sized NRF of 21,000 troops is to be on duty, ready to deploy on short notice. Meanwhile, another NRF force will be going through advanced training and exercises to prepare for its upcoming tour of duty. Concurrently, a third NRF that has recently completed its tour will be standing down. Thus, at any moment, three different NRFs will be operating to one degree or another, but for different purposes. Each NRF is to be composed of multinational NATO forces, with the exact mix to be determined by national contributions and operational requirements. For example, one NRF might be manned largely by British and Dutch forces, and another by French and Italian forces. The NRF is a volunteer posture. It is meant to provide opportunities for participation to all NATO members who are willing and able to meet its operational requirements. The composition of each NRF posture might vary from one duty cycle to the next, thus enabling many European militaries to participate over the course of a few years.

The NRF will draw its combat and support assets mainly from NATO High Readiness Forces: the pool of forces that includes the ARRC, the Eurocorps, the German-Dutch Corps, and other top-tier ground, air, and naval formations. Thus, it will employ only forces that already are strongly committed to NATO integrated command,

and it will not interfere with other European military priorities. While the NRF is to be mostly an all-European force, the United States will need to commit assets in such important enabling categories as C4ISR, strategic mobility, defense suppression, and logistics until the Europeans become self-sufficient in these areas. The NRF will be assigned to the new Allied Command Operations (ACO), with operational command rotating among its two new Joint Force Commands (JFC's) and one maritime Joint Force Headquarters. The effect will be to make all three commands skilled at employing the NRF and engaging in expeditionary strike operations.

The NRF is off to a good start. An initial, small version of it will be fielded in 2003 with an emphasis on SOF assets. Many European countries, including France, have committed to joining the NRF as it is fielded. Whether the NRF will meet its 2006 goal of full operational capability, however, is uncertain. The requisite air and naval forces seem likely to be fielded, but ground forces may be a different matter because of changes that must be made in many areas. The NRF needs to be a properly transformed force with the requisite technologies, networks, and digitization required to perform its missions alongside U.S. forces. As the NRF comes to life, care must be taken to ensure that operational readiness is its first priority. Otherwise, it might fall victim to a dynamic aimed at including too many forces from too many nations under its mantle, thereby weakening its combat power. Likewise, the NRF should take part in transformation, but not at the expense of participating in so many experimental changes that it loses its focus on being ready to fight wars on short notice.

The NRF's command arrangements also bear watching. Each JFC must have a deployable Joint Task Force Headquarters that can command the NRF on distant battlefields. Another issue is the U.S. role. While the United States initially should provide support in critical enabling areas, the Europeans should be encouraged to acquire self-sufficiency in them as soon as possible. In the long run, the NRF should become a mainly European force with the United States contributing on a normal rotating basis. If the NRF becomes dominated by the United States and Britain, its purpose will have been defeated. Likewise, if the NRF is populated by forces from countries that might refuse to participate in its missions at the moment of need, its credibility will be compromised. Whether the NRF needs an opt-out clause can be debated, but opting-in by making firm commitments must be the dominating imperative. For these reasons, NRF success cannot be taken for granted. It will need careful management attention from senior NATO political and military leaders for the foreseeable future.

Preparing a NATO Defense Transformation Roadmap

Prague's decision to create an Allied Command Transformation (ACT) in dual-hat status with the U.S. Joint Forces Command (JFCOM) is a major innovation. It offers the promise of bringing U.S. expertise to bear in focusing and accelerating European transformation for expeditionary warfare. If ACT is to succeed, it must be given a major role not only in exploring new ideas, but also in ensuring that, as European forces train and exercise with U.S. forces, they learn new operational concepts. The more fundamental challenge, however, is to ensure that NATO defense transformation is guided by a sound intellectual vision and a powerful program of coordinated measures to ensure that it succeeds on schedule. The PCC can help in this regard, but it needs to be supplemented by a NATO Defense Transformation Roadmap. It also needs to be supplemented by an Istanbul Summit "Transformation Reinvestment Commitment" to apply savings from European force reductions to enhanced investments in readiness and modernization for the forces that remain.

Although fielding the NRF will be NATO's top priority, the PCC's progress deserves support. The original impetus behind the PCC was to slim down and prioritize the DCI, which allegedly was bulging with its five major categories and 54 specific measures. When the PCC emerged, however, it was even bigger than the DCI, with eight major categories and 450 accompanying measures. The eight categories include such measures as C4ISR, WMD defense, interoperability, information superiority, combat effectiveness, mobility, sustainment, and logistics. Their main effect is to provide NATO leaders with a useful top-down view of force improvements. Meanwhile, the many accompanying measures provide a bottom-up perspective that NATO members can use to develop specific programs. NATO has created a special committee of two Assistant Secretaries General to monitor the PCC with a view toward focusing it on the NRF. Progress on this goal is being briefed every three weeks to the NAC.

Only a few months after its adoption, the PCC already seems in trouble because, for predictable reasons, it is making slow progress. Critics are dismayed, but the truth is that the PCC is a sensible creation, provided that its limited role is kept in mind and a sense of realism guides expectations. The PCC is another in a long line of NATO efforts that focus on functional categories of military activity rather than forces and missions. It was preceded by the Long-Term Defense Plan (LTDP) of the 1970s, the Conventional Defense Initiative (CDI) of the 1980s, and the DCI of the 1990s, all of which used functional categories to generate a detailed look at European forces in key areas. By spelling out a host of worthy NATO-wide improvement measures covering all members, the PCC provides a valuable instrument for helping guide NATO force goals, resource guidance, and country plans. Nor is it too large and encompassing as a tool for broad-scale program and budget management. Comparable Pentagon tools, such as the FYDP and Service POMs, are bigger and include even more measures. But because it is so big and wide-ranging, the PCC is not a good tool for focusing on key forces and top strategic priorities and for propelling NATO transformation forward.

What is to be done? The answer is not to junk the PCC or ratchet it downward. Nor is the answer to try to bolster NATO Ministerial Guidance, which is too vague and general to guide the specifics of force development. Nor are better NATO Force Goals the answer because they result in a dissipated appraisal of NATO individual members in ways that often see only parts of the whole, not the whole itself. All of these long-standing instruments of NATO military planning help provide a comprehensive overview of many endeavors by a huge alliance, but they do not provide an intense focus on new force-building efforts or transformation. Indeed, their main effect is to encourage a business-as-usual emphasis on incremental change, not bold leaps into the future.

To solve this problem, NATO should follow the Pentagon's example by writing its own Defense Transformation Roadmap. Confronted by ponderous FYDP's and POMs, senior Pentagon leaders instructed each Service to write a focused roadmap spelling out how they propose to pursue transformation and to set their priorities accordingly. The resulting roadmaps were initial creations, but they helped focus attention on the meaning, essence, and prospects for U.S. military transformation. In particular, they helped highlight not only where the Services are succeeding, but also where they can do more to pursue transformation jointly and where troubles are likely to be encountered. As a result, U.S. defense transformation now has a better sense of direction and purpose, and senior leaders are better-equipped to guide it.

A NATO transformation roadmap can help perform the same function for the Alliance. As the U.S. experience shows, the process of preparing such a roadmap will encourage NATO and the Europeans to review, revise, and integrate their defense plans and programs. Such a roadmap should provide meaningful guidance, not vague abstractions. It should identify key strategy goals and operational concepts for guiding transformation. It should focus on outputs: the forces and capabilities of old and new members that will be needed to perform each major strategic mission. It should show how NATO members can act individually and collectively to field the necessary forces and capabilities. It should portray budget requirements and force development priorities. It should identify the types of transformation initiatives that are needed, including new weapons and technologies, new doctrines, and new structures. It should encourage innovation and experimentation. Without pretending to design a fixed blueprint, it should establish an evolving transformation strategy for the near-term, mid-term, and long-term. A mid-term focus is particularly important because it provides a connecting bridge between the tangible near-term and the foggy long-term.

Above all, a NATO transformation roadmap should establish clear strategic goals and priorities. Today, NATO's urgent task is not border defense and peacekeeping in absence of anything else, but instead, as MC 317/1 says, becoming better-prepared to conduct joint expeditionary warfare. An expeditionary war involves a journey for a specific purpose to a distant place outside Europe. It requires NATO forces that can deploy swiftly, operate jointly, and strike lethally. Because NATO lacks such assets, its transformation roadmap should focus on fielding the NRF as quickly as possible. The transformation roadmap should specify the NRF assets that must be acquired, a NATO program for acquiring them, the coordinated roles to be played by country plans, and tasks for common NATO investments and the integrated command.

Once such an NRF program is established, a NATO transformation roadmap can address how to improve and transform other high-priority forces. Because NATO HRF forces will provide NRF assets and otherwise be important for power projection, they should be treated not as static legacy assets, but as candidates for transformation in the mid-term. Gradually modernizing the HRF forces with new weapons and doctrines is necessary, but new organizational structures also should be examined. This especially is the case for ground forces. In the Information Age, ponderous divisions and corps with massive logistic support tails need to give way to smaller, agile, and modular formations with lighter support. The U.S. military needs to change in this area, and so do European forces. Simply stated, expeditionary wars will not need the big sustainment assets needed for the Cold War. Recognition of this new-era reality can help pave the way toward high-leverage innovations at affordable cost.

Likewise, the campaigns in Afghanistan and Iraq show that U.S. and European militaries will need improved assets for post-war occupation, stabilization, and reconstruction. European forces are a natural for these important missions, but not to the exclusion of remaining well-prepared for combat. Some observers mistakenly judge that continental European forces should focus on peacekeeping missions while relying upon high-tech U.S. and British forces to do the war fighting. This prescription is wrong because it underestimates what European forces can achieve and would perpetuate an unhealthy division of labor. During the Cold War, many European militaries were highly proficient at combat operations. They can be made fully capable of modern-era combat if they merely acquire new assets and doctrines in achievable ways. Similar to the U.S. military, European militaries can be capable of both winning wars and winning the peace afterward. While pursuing sensible role specialization, a transformation roadmap should point European forces in this twin-hat direction.

A NATO transformation roadmap should pay attention to other military forces and capabilities for old and new members, including counterterrorism, missile defense, and establishing a network of bases, facilities, and schools for helping the new ATC perform its job. But once this goal is accomplished, a transformation roadmap should set stiff priorities by showing how NATO members can economize to extract greater strategic mileage from their defense budgets.

Accordingly, it should call for major reductions in European border defense forces that no longer have critical roles in NATO defense strategy or other important national missions. Today, only 10-20% of European ground forces can deploy outside their borders. A transformation roadmap could endorse reductions of 30-40% in existing European force structures while shifting toward deployable forces. This step would reduce Europe's forces to about 1.6 million military personnel, 35 divisions, 2100 tactical combat aircraft, and 200 naval combatants. Ample forces would remain for performing NATO missions and national missions.

The advantage of such a steep reduction is that it could free large funds—$20 billion or more annually—for investments. As a result, European spending on research, development, and procurement could increase by 50 per cent, thereby propelling transformation forward at a significantly faster pace. The Europeans would have more funds for spending not only on the NRF and other combat forces, but also on homeland security and missile defense, both of which are important priorities. Such an intensified transformation will be possible, however, only if the funds freed from force reductions are retained in national defense budgets. A NATO transformation roadmap should endorse this budgetary strategy as the sine qua non for Alliance health. Its goal should be to convince European governments and parliaments to embrace the prospect of bolstering NATO military preparedness without driving defense budgets through the ceiling, rather than trying to capitalize on a new peace dividend that would not bring peace at all. At the Istanbul summit, NATO leaders could issue a pledge to reinvest for transformation. An "Transformation Reinvestment Commitment" would be a logical partner to the "Prague Capability Commitment" provided both are focused on transformation, the NRF, and other top force priorities.

Designing a New U.S. Military Presence in Europe

With the United States now poised to begin altering its military presence in Europe as part of a global reshuffle, the act of ensuring that a sensible presence emerges is a final priority for NATO defense transformation agenda. For the United States, the goal should not be to punish long-standing allies for their opposition to the Iraq war, but instead to craft a new European presence that supports both U.S.

defense strategy and NATO strategic priorities. This goal can be accomplished, but only if care is taken along the way. The United States needs to act wisely after consulting with NATO and its members, and European countries will need to have a proper understanding of the reasons why they should support changes that are forthcoming. The core reason for change is that while the status quo is a recipe for stagnation, a newly designed U.S. presence can be a vehicle for leading NATO toward an era of relevance and performance.

Today's officially declared U.S. military presence in Europe is about 110,000 troops. This number, however, is not always what it seems. It does not include troops on peacekeeping duty in the Balkans or the 10,000-20,000 sailors and marines aboard the CVBGs and ARGs that regularly patrol the Mediterranean. Today's typical presence thus is about 130,000 troops: somewhat higher than the roughly 100,000 troops deployed in Asia. In addition, the U.S. military commitment to NATO and Europe is measured not only by peacetime presence, but also by other forces that would deploy to Europe in a war. In the Kosovo War, for example, large U.S. air and naval forces converged on the scene. Counting forces in both categories—peacetime presence and wartime reinforcement—the total U.S. military commitment to NATO and Europe is about 350,000 troops. This total commitment seems unlikely to change appreciably so long as a legitimate NATO requirement exists for it. What is mutating today is not this total commitment, but merely the portion permanently stationed in Europe.

Designing an effective future U.S. presence in Europe begins with remembering why the current presence was chosen a decade ago. When the Clinton Administration took power in early 1993, it inherited a presence of 150,000 troops—well down from the Cold War posture of 330,000 troops. The Administration decided to reduce this presence to 100,000 troops. Of this number, fully two-thirds were stationed in Germany at old Cold War bases, and the remaining troops were mainly based in Britain and Italy. The reason for retaining 100,000 troops in Europe was not because this figure had special meaning, but because this number was needed to field the forces deemed necessary for political and military reasons.

A posture of this size enabled the United States to deploy a balanced, multi-mission force of sizable headquarters staffs, four heavy Army brigades stationed in Germany, two or three USAF fighter wings, and Navy bases in the Mediterranean supporting 6th Fleet operations. These forces enabled the U.S. military to maintain its influence in NATO, to preserve a hedge against reappearance of threats to alliance borders, to prepare for new mobile missions as mandated by NATO then-existing strategic concepts, and to conduct training and exercises with allied forces. Since then, the U.S. force presence has been altered in minor ways, such as deployment of a light Army brigade and more prepositioned equipment in Italy. But for the most part, the U.S. presence has stayed remarkably constant, even though NATO, Europe, and the entire world have changed a great deal. Recognizing the need for fresh thinking, DOD's Quadrennial Defense Review of 2001 called for a new approach to global overseas presence in Europe and elsewhere. But apart from suggesting redeployment of some ships to the Persian Gulf and elsewhere, it left the details of the future European presence to further studies. Such studies are now underway.

Today, new strategic priorities are altering the calculations taking place in the U.S. government. Because threats to Europe's borders no longer exist and the U.S. military has become better at power projection from the United States, there is no longer a need to station large ground combat forces in Germany, which is now one of Europe's safest regions. Many of these forces could be put to better use elsewhere in ways that will benefit not only the United States and Europe, but Germany as well. New strategic requirements for U.S. forces and missions elsewhere in Europe, however, are emerging. A vital new mission will be to ensure that U.S. forces in Europe can work closely with the NRF in peace, crisis, and war. Likewise, U.S. forces in Europe must remain capable not only of fulfilling their other defense commitments to NATO, but also of deploying off the continent swiftly to carry out operations of their own. The same applies to U.S. bases and facilities in Europe, which should provide hubs for power projection. Another mission will be to signal continued U.S. engagement and leadership of NATO to old and new members in Central and Eastern Europe, as well as in the northern and southern regions. Guarding the Mediterranean and its sea lanes against new threats will remain critical. Yet another mission will be to maintain interoperability between U.S. and European militaries. A final mission will be to help keep U.S. and NATO defense transformation on parallel tracks.

All of these missions should be taken into account in designing the future U.S. military presence in Europe. Together, these missions suggest that while this presence can be smaller than now, the United States should take care not to reduce too far. The future presence should be neither tiny nor purely symbolic. It will depend in part on the size of U.S. force deployments in the Gulf region. The U.S. forces that remain should disperse outward from current bases in Germany to occupy positions in Eastern Europe and along the southern region: locations where new-era requirements are growing to perform both multinational integration and power projection missions. The United States will no longer require four Army brigades in Germany, but it likely will need two clusters of ground forces in Europe. One cluster should be composed of heavy forces in Northern Europe for promoting NATO interoperability and transformation. The other cluster should be composed of light forces in Italy and elsewhere in southern Europe for swift power projection to the Middle East and other regions. The same calculus applies to designing U.S. air forces in Europe: current bases in Germany (e.g., at Ramstein), Britain, Italy, and elsewhere will remain valuable. As for U.S. naval forces, existing bases and facilities will still be needed to support the 6th Fleet, but its Mediterranean deployments may be smaller than during the past, and in any event, likely will vary as a function of changing conditions.

What do these imperatives mean when they are added up? Future manpower levels will need to be determined on the basis of analysis, but the more important consideration is the type of U.S. forces deployed, their locations, and their missions. Manpower levels should stem from these considerations, not the other way around. Indeed, the manpower level may be a variable, not a constant. The future U.S. presence will rely more heavily than now on forward operating locations and prepositioned equipment rather than fixed bases occupied by stationed forces. During times of training and exercises, U.S.-based forces will temporarily deploy to Europe, thereby elevating manpower well-above normal levels. After they leave, troop strength will recede until the next deployment cycle. Regardless of their manpower levels, the forces that remain in Europe, or are newly deployed there, should be designed to support U.S. interests and to help enhance NATO strategic effectiveness. Provided this is the case, the new U.S. presence may be smaller and significantly altered, but it can be a powerful instrument for pursuing a bright future for the Alliance.

The Second Track: Pursuing Political Transformation for Strategic Realignment

For all its importance, a vigorous NATO defense transformation agenda will lack a compelling strategic purpose and will not be fully effective unless it is accompanied by the second part of a dual-track strategy: NATO political transformation for strategic realignment. Whereas the Afghanistan war demonstrated NATO need for defense transformation, the war in Iraq highlighted NATO's need for strategic realignment by exposing fault-lines that can cripple the alliance's ability to act in politically unified ways outside Europe. Defense transformation is unlikely to succeed unless political transformation also occurs, and vice-versa. These two enterprises thus go hand in hand.

What does "strategic realignment" mean? Basically, it means a process of change by which the Alliance enhances its political-military capacity to project power and purpose southward into the Greater Middle East and adjoining areas. As stated earlier, strategic realignment can best be pursued through the following four-fold agenda that, along with defense transformation, will produce a more unified and effective Atlantic Alliance:

• Creating a common vision of threat perceptions, goals, strategy, and standards for using military force

• Reforming NATO decisionmaking to create greater flexibility and responsiveness for handling security issues outside Europe.

• Organizing NATO forces for stabilization and reconstruction operations.

• Creating a new Partnership for Cooperation in the Greater Middle East.

These four measures should be seen not only on their individual merits, but also in terms of their combined impact. The first two measures aim at strengthening NATO political capacity to forge united and effective policies for the Middle East and other regions. In the aftermath of the Iraq debate, opportunities have opened for the United States and Britain to work closely with Spain, Italy, Poland, and other new members. Whether the "Quad" can be recreated is to be seen, but NATO clearly cannot function effectively if the United

States and Britain are always at loggerheads with Germany and France in ways leaving other members torn between them. The first measure of creating a common vision aims at bringing these four leaders closer together so that NATO will be better able to act as a unified alliance. Conversely, the second measure of reforming NATO decision-making aims to provide the Atlantic Alliance with the flexibility to act when lack of unanimous consensus threatens the capacity of mission-responsible countries to defend common interests.

Whereas these two measures address NATO internal politics, the last two measures seek to enhance NATO performance for situations other than war-fighting. Obviously NATO needs the ability to fight wars at long distances. The defense transformation measures discussed earlier will provide the requisite capabilities and are a part of strategic realignment. Yet NATO will be a limited alliance if it can only fight wars but do little else. It also needs a better capacity to address post-war situations and to become active in the Middle East in peacetime. The third measure aims to provide NATO with a stronger role in post-war situations, such as the stabilization and reconstruction of Iraq. The fourth measure creates a peacetime outreach program, similar to NATO Partnership for Peace (PFP) in Eastern Europe that would pursue improved ties to friendly Middle East militaries. Together, these four measures are intended to strengthen NATO cohesion and performance in mutually reinforcing ways. If they are all adopted, along with a robust set of military measures, they will produce a new Atlantic Alliance that is strategically realigned in the best sense of that term.

Writing a New Harmel Report to Help Establish a Common Strategic Vision

The damaging confrontation over Iraq makes the importance of this measure crystal clear. The Atlantic Alliance badly needs to forge a common strategic vision that will narrow the cavernous gap between the United States and key European countries—especially Germany and France—on the issues surrounding the use of strategic power outside Europe. Otherwise, similar confrontations may erupt in the future, and the next one could destroy NATO, not merely damage it. The term "common strategic vision" does not mean that the United States and Europe must agree on everything. But it does mean that they must agree on the strategic basics, possess a shared framework for cooperative action, and respect each other in areas where disagreements still exist.

Some observers judge that now is not the time to debate these issues. Their understandable reason is fear that a high-profile debate will do more harm than good by widening the gap in visions rather than narrowing it. They argue that since an eerie calm has settled over NATO in the aftermath of Iraq, the prudent choice is to let wounds heal. Today's calm in Brussels, however, is illusory. The bitter divide on strategic policy is not caused by differences at NATO Headquarters, where most people think alike and want to keep NATO alive. Instead, the divide is caused by sharply differing views in national capitals, the media, and public opinion. Ignoring the divide will not close it. It will reappear with the next crisis. The only way to lessen it is to grapple with the core issues in ways that produce a better transatlantic understanding .

The bitter flare-up over Iraq occurred because a gap-closing dialogue had not taken place earlier. Such a dialogue was attempted in 1999 when the new NATO strategic concept was adopted at the Washington Summit, but this compromise document largely papered over unresolved differences that lay hidden for the next three years and surfaced at the United Nations. The terrorism of Sept. 11, 2001, exacerbated the problem by deeply alarming the United States while leaving Europe less worried. Because the current interlude between crises may be temporary, it may be a last opportunity to resolve these issues before they can no longer be addressed in a civil manner. The gap between Americans and Europeans is not so great that it cannot be closed or at least appreciably narrowed. The United States grasps that the use of military force in the Middle East and elsewhere must be tempered by mature political judgment and respect for international law. The Bush Administration has made clear that it anticipates no additional wars in the Middle East, that it will use diplomacy to address remaining problems, and that military force will be a last resort. Most European governments grasp that sometimes military power must be used against dangerous threats arising from these regions. The EU report by Javier Solana on "A Secure Europe for a Better World" provides a good basis for a sensible dialogue. Many European foreign ministers acknowledge that on occasions of imminent threat, preventive war sometimes is necessary. The grounds for a meeting of minds exist by forging a sensible a blend of these positions.

Confidence in success also comes from history. This is not the first time NATO has been divided. Indeed, stiff debates arose during the Cold War. An especially bitter debate erupted in the early 1960s when the United States wanted to shift NATO defense strategy from massive retaliation to flexible response, and the Europeans resisted out of fear this step would weaken deterrence. The debate resulted in Germany threatening to develop nuclear weapons and France leaving the integrated command. But it was finally resolved when Americans and Europeans rolled up their sleeves, began talking calmly, and showed the patience to analyze the complex issues carefully. They eventually agreed upon a new strategy of flexible response that bolstered conventional forces but preserved the option to climb the ladder of nuclear escalation if the initial defense failed. The common strategy adopted by them proved to be highly successful. It laid the foundation for NATO growing defense strength that helped win the Cold War. A successful outcome of this sort is possible again if the Alliance merely recalls its own history and its mechanisms for consensus-formation.

Exactly what is to be done? How can the Alliance transform the bruised feelings and deep suspicions over Iraq into a constructive dialogue that results in a meeting of minds? The answer is not for NATO to engage in an official study, for this step could result in many governments digging deeper into entrenched positions. A better idea is to prepare a new Harmel Report akin to the original report written in 1967. Such a report would be written by a team of independent European and American thinkers. They would have the freedom to examine the issues outside the glare of publicity and pressures from their governments. When their judgments and recommendations were finalized, NATO would be free to accept, reject, or modify them. The good features of their analysis could be adopted as official policy to help harmonize American and European perspectives.

The Harmel Report was named after Belgian Foreign Minister Pierre Harmel, who proposed the idea. It sought to blend detente with deterrence and defense in ways that maintained NATO solidarity. It was commissioned in early 1967 and written over a period of six months. Although it was conducted under the auspices of NATO

Secretary General, its four sub-groups were led by senior rapporteurs from outside NATO, who spoke for themselves and did not take official instructions from their governments. When their final report was issued, it was reviewed by NATO headquarters and national capitals. Many of its arguments were adopted by NATO ministers in December 1967, and the entire document was issued as an annex to their communiqué. As the logic of the Harmel Report became established throughout NATO in the following months, the effect was to help provide the Alliance with stronger footing for handling a troubled future.

Today, a new Harmel Report could be drafted using a similar procedure. Its goal should not be a bland compromise that submerges differences, but an intelligent blend of American and European views that resolves these differences and produces coherent strategic concepts acceptable to both sides of the Atlantic. The EU Solana report takes future threats seriously and calls upon the EU to play an assertive role in global security affairs in partnership with the United States. Although Solana's study does not put forth an agenda for NATO, it could become a launch pad for a group of European and American wise-men to do so.

What issues should the new Harmel Report address? First, it should focus on establishing a common definition of future threats. Whereas today the United States is deeply worried about threats posed by terrorists, tyrants, and WMD proliferation, Europe has less fear of them. If a shared understanding of threats can be forged, the United States and Europe will have a stronger basis for acting jointly and be better able to elicit support from parliaments and publics. However, it must offer more than an intelligence estimate. It must also provide a coherent sense of common goals, strategies, and actions not only for combating these threats but also for eradicating the conditions that generate them. Thus, it must address how the United States and Europe should work together to promote democracy and markets across the Middle East and elsewhere.

Likewise, a new Harmel Report should forge a common understanding of the strategic roles that the United States and Europe are to play in carrying burdens and accepting responsibility in the coming years. It should aim for a relationship in which both sides work together in exercising soft and hard power, rather than rely upon a dysfunctional division of labor in which Europe provides the soft power and the United States the hard power. Finally, it must help forge a shared understanding of standards for employing military force against threats. Many Europeans cling to the Westphalian concept that military power should be employed only after aggression has occurred. By contrast, the United States has adopted a new doctrine of preventive war when threats are "grave, gathering, and imminent." NATO cannot survive in the face of a militant America and a pacifist Europe. A similar mindset on this critical issue is vital if NATO is to remain united in the coming years. If this difficult issue is discussed sensibly, an alliance-wide standard for going to war can be found.

A new Harmel Report need not result in a NATO strategy that either hamstrings the United States or compels Europeans to blindly support decisions from Washington. Instead, it can help ensure that the United States and Europe work closely more often to strike a wise synthesis of restraint and the muscular use of power. Before and after a new Harmel Report is written, both sides of the Atlantic can take other steps to encourage a respectful dialogue. The United States can do a better job of consulting with European governments. It also can mount a public relations campaign to explain its foreign policy to Europeans, including its many still-important contributions in Europe. Meanwhile, Germany and France can rediscover the importance of acting as counterparts of the United States and Britain, not counterweights. Other European governments can do a better job of explaining the benefits of cooperating with the United States to their publics in ways that counter the simplistic, erroneous messages often conveyed in their media. Such steps would help cool the temperature of what has become a fevered relationship, thereby allowing calm heads to prevail.

Reforming NATO Decision-Making

Even with a common strategic vision, making decisions to project NATO power into distant areas does not promise to be easy. During the Cold War, NATO possessed consensus behind defense plans for responding quickly to aggression against its borders. In the current era, swift responses may also be needed against threats that emerge outside NATO borders, and even normal peacetime activities often will not permit extended delays. Difficulties will especially arise when gray-area situations create legitimate debates over how best to respond. Such situations typically take place under Article 4, when the use of NATO power is discretionary, rather than under Article 5, when alliance borders are threatened and using military power is virtually mandatory. In such situations, NATO must be able to perform two key functions: to debate options thoroughly and then to act decisively. NATO today is good at the former, but not the latter.

Most democracies value both debate and action. This is why they make most policy decisions by majority rule, not unanimous votes, which are a prescription for paralysis because dissent is inevitable. NATO, however, is not a normal democracy in this regard. Today's problem is that France and Germany oppose key features of how the United States and Britain are acting in Iraq. But a big underlying problem will remain, even if these four countries patch up their current differences. The problem is that NATO is a big alliance with a proclivity to act only when its members unanimously agree on the action. Because NATO already has 19 members and will soon have 26, unanimity could become a scarce commodity in the years ahead.

True, a single, stubborn country will normally be hard-pressed to use its veto power to block NATO action. But as the debate over defending Turkey in the weeks before invasion of Iraq showed, a small group of dissenting countries can cause serious problems. While the Turkey problem was ultimately solved, in the future such a group could prevail in damaging ways by stubbornly standing its ground. The risk is that NATO will be plunged into paralysis when assertive activity and regular gear-shifting are needed. When unanimity does not exist, NATO could be prevented from responding in crises and wars. Equally bad, mission-responsible countries—those willing to accept responsibility for performing demanding missions outside Europe—will lack the peacetime authority to work with the integrated command to prepare the forces and plans that must be invoked in crises. If advance preparations are not made, quick and decisive NATO action at the moment of truth may be impossible even if members unanimously agree to act. This risk is not hypothetical and futuristic: it already exists in spades because the integrated command cannot prepare full-scale plans and programs unless the NAC unanimously authorizes it to do so in each case.

NATO possesses finessing mechanisms that can help circumvent the unanimity rule on occasion, but all of them are thin reeds to rely upon in today's world. One finessing mechanism is the "silence procedure" whereby a member who disagrees with a widespread consensus chooses to abstain from voting, thereby allowing the consensus to carry the day. Another mechanism is to shift decisionmaking from the NAC to the Defense Planning Committee (DPC). This allows NATO to make decisions without France, which belongs to the NAC but not the DPC. A third mechanism is for the Secretary General to claim to speak for a unanimous consensus without taking a formal vote. This mechanism was employed in the Kosovo war and helped enable NATO to conduct military operations even though some members had misgivings. A fourth mechanism is that SACEUR and other commanders can prepare informal defense plans.

The problem with these finessing mechanisms is that they only work sometimes and can easily be overturned by a small number of members intent on having their way. Such members can refuse to stay silent, can insist the NAC be used, can deny the Secretary General the authority to speak for NATO, and can block NATO military commanders from planning informally.

Today's situation requires decision processes that are more flexible and responsive. NATO can gauge how to create them by recalling its history. The use of unanimous voting is a recent practice. It began in the early 1990s, when France was objecting to emerging NATO policies in the Balkans, and the Alliance wanted France and others on board for this new out-of-area operation. During the Cold War, NATO employed unanimity when making major decisions about core strategic concepts or such controversial nuclear matters as deployment of Pershing II and GLCM missiles. But in conventional defense planning, NATO acted differently. It wisely delegated considerable authority to those countries that were mainly responsible for key missions in different areas. For example, it permitted the nine countries responsible for defending FRG borders to carry out their important business without interference from other members. The same practice applied in the north Atlantic, northern Europe, and southern Europe, where defense plans and forces were built by even smaller coalitions of responsible contributors. The bottom line is that NATO has shown flexibility in the past, and there is nothing in the Washington Treaty that mandates unanimous voting practices.

What can be done to create more flexibility in ways that avoid paralysis yet preserve healthy debate and widespread consensus-formation? The guiding principle should be to craft new decision procedures whereby members who regularly accept responsibility for new-era missions are granted reasonable discretionary authority to act in proper ways yet are still subjected to scrutiny by the rest of the alliance to ensure that they are acting wisely. An initial step toward this model can be taken by allowing the Secretary General to authorize the integrated command in peacetime to prepare contingency plans for potential contingencies. The Secretary General could take this step in response to requests from a threatened member, from SACEUR, or from members that could be called upon to perform NATO missions outside Europe. These planning activities would be supervised by the Secretary General and the Military Committee. Provided they are consistent with NATO strategic concepts and Ministerial Guidance, they could not be vetoed by the NAC and DPC. Likewise, NATO military leaders would be authorized to prepare the necessary forces under the Secretary General's guidance by using the standard force-building process in consultation with participating members. These steps would have the advantage of enabling NATO to prepare for future responses, thereby helping ensure that the Alliance has the necessary wherewithal when the need arises.

Along with this practice, a bigger step would be to depart from the unanimity principle at the NAC for making decisions in crises. While alternatives need to be studied, a sensible model might be a variation on U.N. Security Council decisionmaking. The Security Council gives veto power only to its five permanent members. When these five members agree, it seeks only majority support from the Council as a whole, which has ten non-permanent members. The Council does not have a reputation for impulsive conduct, but unlike NATO, it can act in the face of limited internal dissent, and it has done so in the past. If NATO adopts such a model, it should not create "permanent members" who always have veto power. Instead, it should grant veto power only to those members who regularly commit substantial resources and efforts to each key mission. When these countries agree to act in their area of responsibility—for example, by using the NRF—voting by the rest of the NAC would be conducted by majority rule or a two-thirds rule. Normally, this practice would mean that a solid NAC majority of 15-20 members must vote in favor of an action. Such a practice would ensure review by the NAC, yet allow for action even if a few countries disagree.

Perhaps this U.N.-like model could be applied to the NRF and, if it proved its worth, be expanded to other NATO forces and bigger operations. This model does not imply creation of a single coalition of members for carrying out all actions. Most likely, it would result in multiple coalitions or "committees of contributors", each of which would handle a different mission or region.[1] These coalitions would vary in composition, size, and orientation. A coalition handling North Africa might differ from one handling the Persian Gulf. Often, the United States and Britain would lead these coalitions, but not always. Regardless, all NATO members would be welcome to belong to the coalitions of their choice. But to join as a full-fledged member, a country would be required to commit significant resources and to prove its mettle as a worthy, reliable partner. Its influence within the coalition would be a function of its resource commitments and its willingness to accept responsibility for missions.

This model is not a prescription for liberating the United States and Britain from the shackles of Germany and France, who still could recruit supporters when they dissent. Moreover, if these or other countries want veto authority, they merely must establish demonstrated track-records of accepting responsibility in the mission-areas of their choice. Germany, France, and other countries thus would be free to participate in missions of importance to them and would wield substantial influence over how these missions are handled. Indeed, they may find themselves leading some NATO missions and thereby value their enhanced discretionary authority.

Would the United States lose its veto power? The answer is that if it wants veto power, it merely needs to be a leading contributor to missions of its choice. In most cases of NATO power projection, the United States will be such a contributor. What about the matter of identifying who should possess veto power within each coalition? To prevent countries from making small contributions to gain veto power with disruptive purposes in mind, a standard should be established whereby veto power is granted only to those members who make significant contributions and establish consistent track records for responsible conduct. Such standards were applied in the Cold War.

---

[1] The "Committee of Contributors" model is developed in Leo G. Michel, "NATO Decisionmaking: Au Revoir to the Consensus Rule?" *Strategic Forum* 202, (Washington, DC: National Defense University Press, August 2003).

When France withdrew from the integrated command, it lost its right to major influence over NATO forward defense plans even though it still made forces conditionally available for rear-area roles. By contrast, the FRG and other members maintained their influence at high levels because they never flagged in their forward defense duties.

The following chart summarizes how these changes would produce a new style of NATO decisionmaking. Yes, this process would be more complex than the current practice of unanimity across the board. NATO still would require unanimity for such encompassing decisions as its strategic concept, core goals, strategy inside and outside Europe, decisions to admit new members, and generic standards for using military force. But it would have greater flexibility to prepare contingency plans and engage in necessary pre-crisis force preparations. When crises erupt, it would make decisions in a manner similar to the U.N. Security Council, and thus would have greater flexibility in handling them. It no longer would face the type of paralysis that threatens its relevance and effectiveness.

Changes to NATO Decision-Making

NATO Decisions	Cold War	Today	Future
Contingency Planning	Continuous	NAC-Directed	SACEUR-Authorized with Oversight by NATO Secretary General
Force Preparations	Ongoing	NAC-Directed	NATO Secretary General-Authorized Through Consultations with Members
Crisis Response	When Attacked	NAC-Directed	U.N. Security Council Model
Overall Process	Automatic	Road-Blocked	Flexible and Responsive

Involving NATO in Post-War Stabilization and Reconstruction

Creating a common strategic vision and adopting flexible decision-making processes will strengthen the Atlantic Alliance for the years ahead. But concrete steps are also needed to broaden NATO activities in the Middle East and elsewhere for the near-term. What can be done? Decisions in this arena should be guided by the principle that NATO must become an alliance that has a full spectrum of capabilities.

When the time is right, NATO clearly should become involved in the post-war task of stabilizing and reconstructing Iraq. Performing this task seemingly will require a sizable military presence for a considerable time. Today, the United States is contributing most of the forces for this duty, yet it will face strong pressures to trim its presence in the months ahead. Britain, Poland, and other NATO countries are already present in significant numbers, but larger European forces will be needed. If the NATO integrated command is called upon to help, it could provide the leadership architecture needed to guide multinational forces.

In addition, NATO should broaden its thinking beyond Iraq. Crises and wars that mandate NATO participation may occur elsewhere. As a result, NATO should develop a better organized standing capacity to perform stabilization and reconstruction (S&R) missions. They involve such activities as securing still-troubled zones, establishing police forces and the rule of law, restoring public services in electrical power, water and sewage, repairing damaged bridges and roads, cleaning up war destruction, and building democratic governments. These diverse functions require specialized military and civilian assets such as military police, construction engineers, medical personnel, and civil administrators. European militaries and governments possess such assets. New NATO members could make major contributions. But these assets need to be organized so that they are ready when needed. NATO can work with members to prepare for such missions by either the integrated command or ad-hoc coalitions.

Some Americans blanch at the idea of NATO becoming regularly involved in S&R missions. They fear a loss of U.S. influence and bungled operations. In this arena, however, NATO already has proven its mettle in the Balkans and is now taking over the ISAF mission in Afghanistan. In Iraq, much will depend upon whether participating NATO members agree upon the strategic goals for reconstruction. In other cases, a common vision will be equally necessary. Provided consensus exists on strategic goals, NATO can be an effective instrument for this important mission.

Creating a Partnership for Cooperation in the Middle East

NATO could helpfully involve itself in peacetime affairs of the Greater Middle East by creating a Partnership for Cooperation (PFC) that would seek to establish constructive relations between NATO and friendly militaries there. NATO already has a "Mediterranean

Dialogue" with some North African countries, but it is mostly confined to diplomatic exchanges and does not cover the entire Middle East and Persian Gulf. A PFC might be part of the existing Partnership for Peace (PFP) in Eastern Europe and surrounding areas. Alternatively, it might be an entirely separate creation, with a mission and administrative staff of its own. The tradeoffs between these two models need to be examined. Expanding upon the PFP would be the simplest, easiest, and least-costly alternative. Yet dealing with the Middle East will be quite different from dealing with Eastern Europe and the former Soviet Union. This argues for a separate effort.

Regardless of the option chosen, a PFC would not be intended to prepare Middle East countries for admission into NATO. Instead, it would aspire to build ties with Middle Eastern militaries in peace-building efforts that strengthen their roles in the war on terrorism, encourage their democratization, familiarize them with the United States and Europe, and enhance their efficiency for self-defense missions. A PFC might provide collaboration in such areas as law enforcement, disrupting terrorist cells, budgeting and programming, peacekeeping, search and rescue, disaster relief, and border control. Such a PFC must be focused on enhancing regional stability, not fostering military competition. The PFC must not endanger the security of any country, including Israel. It could begin small, with such already-friendly countries as Egypt, Jordan, and Gulf Cooperative Council States. Afterward, it could gradually expand to include a widening set of other countries.

A PFC would be intended to initiate a process of growing dialogue and cooperation between NATO and Middle Eastern Countries. This PFC would not be a one-size-fits-all creation. Instead, each participating country would be able to craft a PFC program suited to its tastes, in consultation with NATO members willing to work closely with it. Thus, PFC programs might differ appreciably. The NATO PFP in Eastern Europe pursued flexible arrangements from the onset, which helps account for its considerable success over the past decade. East European countries were able to approach NATO at a scope and pace of their own choosing. The same philosophy would apply to a PFC for the Middle East.

A PFC would be a historic departure for NATO. It would give NATO a valuable new mission and would involve NATO in the visionary task of bringing peace, security, and democracy to a big region that, even after the victory in Iraq, promises to be troubled for years to come. It could begin by taking stock of comparable efforts already being pursued by NATO members that act unilaterally in various Middle Eastern countries. It could ascertain how efforts by additional countries could be added to forge a multinational NATO program with each PFC member. Each PFC member thus would benefit from help provided by a team of NATO countries.

How effective can a PFC be? Especially in its initial stages, it likely will be considerably less effective than was the PFP in Eastern Europe. At the time PFP appeared, East European countries had recently been liberated from communism and the Soviet Union. They were struggling to adopt democracy and market economies. They wanted to join NATO to gain security and the EU to become prosperous. Their militaries wanted collaboration with NATO militaries to adopt new doctrines, weapons, and practices that clearly were better than those of the Warsaw Pact. For all these reasons, their governments wanted to belong to the Western Club, and their publics mostly agreed with them. As a result, many rushed to embrace PFP because it was a vehicle for pursuing these larger goals, not because of specific measures.

Middle Eastern conditions today are vastly different. The Israel-Palestinian conflict could inhibit many Arab governments. Most Arab states are ruled by monarchies or traditional regimes that are chary of democratic reforms, even though they recognize the advantages of adopting market economies. Still animated by nationalism, many governments are also suspicious of western countries, fearing American domination or renewed European imperialism. Their Islamic societies vary in their fundamentalism, but few hold any love for western culture, which is seen as too secular and materialist. Their militaries likely will see significant technical attractions in a PFC that allows them to strengthen their capabilities in useful areas. But they will not want NATO to control their defense strategies and forces, or even to acquire full knowledge of them. These attitudes are impediments to quick success of a PFC.

Whether initial success by a PFC would produce a wholesale shift toward pro-western Arab foreign policies is another matter. NATO members might find themselves laboring in PFC vineyards for a long period while questioning the merits of the enterprise. Yet, gains might be made in such important areas as counter-terrorism and in softening the sharp edges of Islamic fundamentalism. Likewise, PFC might help nudge the Middle East toward greater stability and help plant seeds of democratization. If such gains are achieved, they could make PFC a sound investment even if they do not transform the Middle East in the ways that Eastern Europe has been transformed. As a result, NATO needs to be realistic in its expectations, yet assertive in pursuing an idea that makes sense.

Conclusion

Is this dual-track strategy of political and military transformation for strategic realignment needed by an Atlantic Alliance in deep trouble? Yes. Will it be adopted and will it succeed? That remains to be seen. One thing can be said. Ten years ago, a common refrain was that NATO must "go out-of-area or go out of business." The Alliance responded by moving eastward but not southward. For the good of the United States and Europe, it now needs to move southward. The larger meaning of the war on terrorists and tyrants is that the United States is now coming ashore in the Greater Middle East in a historic attempt to bring peace, democracy, and markets to that troubled region. NATO also needs to do so because the United States cannot handle this ultra-demanding task alone. If NATO fails to respond, this time it truly will go out of business.

Chapter 4

The Consequences of U.S. and NATO Transformation for the European Union: A European View

Yves Boyer

"Transformation" has become the new catch-all word, a new slogan about defense and security affairs in the United States. The problem with slogans is that their appeal does not always match their substance. Their durability in the U.S. Department of Defense is usually a direct function of the political and bureaucratic tenure of those who head the Pentagon.

In a sense, "transformation" addresses the obvious: the military is not isolated from other human activities, which are in a permanent state of flux. Political, cultural, societal, industrial and technological "transformations" have always had a direct impact on military affairs, as demonstrated in many historical examples. With the growing importance of information technologies in post-modern societies, the military cannot escape adapting defense structure, adjusting doctrine and developing new weapon systems in order to maximize the processing and sharing of time urgent information. This is the new prerequisite to plan and execute swift military operations on the digitalized battlefield.

Despite the immediate seductiveness of this notion, which promises to pave the way to a new kind of "Blitzkrieg" for the early 21st century—as implied in military concepts inherent to "transformation" such as Rapid Decisive Operation (RDO)—its multi-faceted nature poses problems for U.S. allies.

On one hand, transformation is aimed at revolutionizing the conception of warfare itself. As such it transcends national boundaries. For Europeans, it is of the greatest importance, from a purely military sense, to understand its implications for defense and develop cooperation with the U.S. NATO is not necessarily the best vehicle for that cooperation. A new multilateral body like the Multinational Interoperability Council (MIC) seems to offer better perspectives for

Germany, the UK and France, the three key West European military players. The three have taken very seriously, from a military viewpoint, the need to remain co-operable with the U.S. when America is embarked in the "transformation" of its military forces and doctrines. Berlin, London and Paris commit significant resources to that goal. For example, the French equivalent of the JCS, the EMA (*Etat-Major des Armées*) is highly engaged in preparing its participation in the MNE3 exercise to be held in the framework of the MIC in early February 2004.[1] This exercise, to be held in the U.S., will be focused on initial preparation and planning for military action against an opponent using new concepts developed in the U.S. within the framework of the transformation process led by the Joint Forces Command. France will be a key player in this exercise.

On the other hand "transformation" is so grounded in American military culture, bureaucratic incentives and political perspectives that many of its concerns, applications and implications outside the U.S. remain potentially very limited. These contrasting views indicate that "transformation" will undoubtedly nurture just as many misunderstandings as elements of convergence between the United States and its European allies.

Transformation: an Endeavor "Made in the USA"

Such an endeavor is, indeed, not disconnected from the political and technological dialectics linking U.S. societal and industrial transformation with military affairs. The debate encouraged by this evolution is not necessarily of universal value. "Transformation" has specific characteristics that do not automatically fit U.S. allies' objectives and needs even if the current experience followed by the U.S. is of great interest.

Skepticism regarding the applicability of U.S. "transformation" to allies is based on experience derived from the debates in the mid 1990s about the notion of a "revolution in military affairs" (RMA). The RMA already called for innovative views of warfare, for transforming military structure and for rapid moves towards planning and conducting military operations. It called for greater reliance on information-based knowledge for almost "perfect" battlefield awareness to

---

[1] MNE3 is part of a series of exercises being done within the framework of the MIC.

implement "dominant maneuver." The idea was exciting. The notion
also became a catch-all term during the mid 1990s. It punctuated most
U.S. military analysis and official speeches at that time. However, the
concept was far too broad in its scope and purpose, and it was not
mature enough. The notion of RMA was thus a source of multiple
interpretations while offering little immediate concrete application to
the U.S. military. It was implicitly acknowledged in the Department
of Defense's 1997 Quadrennial Defense Review that RMA could only
be seen as a new template; it could not, as such, serve as a guide for
immediate transformation of the U.S. defense posture. The notion
was far too vague to be translated into new doctrine, operational concepts, or equipment. It left the services with little concrete orientation. With *Joint Vision 2010* the U.S. Joint Chiefs of Staff brought,
instead, tangible guidance to orient the doctrinal debate and the
acquisition requirements of the services. It put limits on the doctrinal
evolution of each Service by providing each of them with four clear
objectives to enhance jointness for attaining a "full-spectrum dominance"against any type of opponent: dominant maneuver; precision
engagement; focused logistics; and full-dimensional protection.

Whatever discrepancies may exist between the appearance and the
real expectations regarding RMA, European allies were first intrigued
and later "requested" to adjust their force posture to the shift in military affairs apparently being made by the U.S. That was basically the
aim of NATO's DCI (Defense Capabilities Initiative) launched at the
NATO Summit in Washington in April 1999. The ambitions rapidly
faded away, however, and the goals set by the DCI were, for the most
part, never met by the Europeans.

Still, the assumption about the transformation of warfare deriving
from rapid technological evolution, coupled with the imperative to
keep an already huge U.S. military apparatus mobilized and modern-
ized, became an important political issue during the presidential race
in 2000. Candidate George W. Bush made a very strong commitment,
if elected, to "transform" the U.S. military posture. In his speech at
the Citadel he stressed that in military affairs he intended "to force
new thinking and hard choices,", adding "we will skip a generation of
technology."[2] Once in the White House, George W. Bush stuck to his

---

[2] September 23, 1999.

promises and tasked his Defense Secretary to work on "transforming" the U.S. military apparatus. The goals of "transformation" were later encapsulated in the 2001 Quadrennial Defense Review (QDR).[3] This document represented the charter for transforming U.S. forces. "Transformation" was portrayed as being "an endeavor that must be embraced in earnest" and based on four pillars: strengthening joint operations; experimenting with new approaches to warfare, operations, concepts and capabilities; exploiting U.S. military intelligence advantages; and developing transformational capabilities. A few weeks after the release of the QDR the Secretary of Defense highlighted the main characteristics of "transformation" by assigning six transformational goals to the U.S. armed forces: to protect the U.S. homeland and bases overseas; to project and sustain power in distant theaters; to deny enemy sanctuary; to protect U.S. information networks from attack; to use information technology to link up different kinds of U.S. forces; and to maintain unhindered access to space and to protect U.S. space capabilities.[4]

The "Transformed" Transatlantic Scene and Military "Transformation"

Bearing in mind the traditional Clauswitzian adage that even in times of peace (and even among allies), war or in this case evolution of military concepts and doctrines "*is merely the continuation of policy by other means,*" the U.S. insisted that "transformation" rapidly become part of NATO's agenda and thus instrumentalized the concept during a transitional period both for NATO and for ESDP (European Security and Defense Policy).

This is precisely what makes the sheer replication of "transformation" within NATO machinery so difficult. As General Harald Kujat, chairman of NATO's Military Committee, has pointed out: "Can the American Transformation process be exported as it is to NATO? The answer to that is a resounding "no" ....Within NATO the Alliance, transformation cannot follow the same path. When dealing with transformation, NATO must consider a very specific challenge which

---

[3] QDR Report, September 30, 2001.

[4] "21st Century Transformation," Secretary of Defense remarks, National Defense University, Fort McNair, Washington DC, January 31, 2002.

does not encumber U.S. transformers: multinationality of sovereign states."[5] The way "transformation" was initially portrayed to the Europeans created the impression that the stakes transcended military affairs alone, particularly when the vehicle touted to transform NATO forces was the NRF (NATO Response Force), itself tasked with multi-purposed objectives. Indeed, questions regarding the intended purposes of "transformation" could no longer be disconnected from the overall political context of the transatlantic relations. It also could not be disconnected from its potential impact on European armed forces and upon the future of ESDP under the contradictory pressures of transatlantic stagnation as a consequence of the Iraqi crisis and acceleration of European integration by a core group of EU countries.

Accordingly, the first consideration guiding cautious European reactions to the full notion of transformation is related to the current U.S. Administration's views on peace, war and international security. Compared with its predecessor, George W. Bush's Administration is displaying new approaches to international affairs. The first such approach, notably, is a clear move towards unilateralism. The phenomenon is not new. Such a tendency has existed at least since the early 1980s. But President George W. Bush has given this trend new impetus. Even before Bush assumed power, individuals who would later hold key positions in his Administration argued strongly in favor of a new U.S. foreign policy aimed at maximizing U.S. national interests by relying more on U.S. strength than on multilateral mechanisms.[6] Such views caused commentators, particularly in Europe, to fear that unilateralism would increasingly come to characterize U.S. foreign and security policy.[7]

The second consideration is related to preventive war. The publication of the *National Security Strategy of the United States*, in which the White House explicitly emphasized its right of pre-emptive action ("we will not hesitate to act alone, if necessary, to exercise our right of self-defense by acting pre-emptively")[8] raised concerns in many

---

[5] General Harald Kujat, speech at SACLANT's seminar "Open Road," Norfolk, USA January 21, 2003.

[6] See for example, John Bolton, "Should We Take Global Governance Seriously?" *Chicago Journal of International Law*, Vol.1, No. 2, Fall 2000.

[7] See for example the *Financial Times*'s editorial, December 15, 2000.

[8] September 17, 2003.

European capitals and among European public opinion.[9] The new U.S. national strategy was received with great reservation in many countries, and may have dire long-term consequences for the Alliance. As rightly pointed out by Barry Posen, "As preventive war is difficult to sell abroad, this policy requires the ability to act alone militarily—a unilateral global offensive capability. The effort to achieve such a capability will cause unease around the world and will make it increasingly difficult for the United States to find allies."[10]

The Iraqi crisis and its resolution, by and large, epitomized this new U.S. behavior on the international stage. It scared Europe's public opinion, including the publics of "new Europe," and cannot leave unscathed the long-term political relationship between Washington and the Europeans. In Europe it is now a widely held view that the U.S., particularly since 9/11, is pursuing nationalistic and "imperial" goals.[11] Consequently, the idea that the West as such could function in military affairs as a single entity, under U.S. leadership, is challenged. It is challenged, first, by a variety of new developments advancing European integration, which point to a military emancipation from U.S. tutelage on European security. But it is also challenged by a lack of consensus between the two sides of the Atlantic about many aspects of present international life and regulation; as well as by fundamental divergences linked to a transformation of U.S. views regarding the role and place of America in the international community.

There are numerous signs pointing to growing European hesitancy about blindly following the U.S. European unease was apparent during *Dynamic Response 07*, a crisis management study seminar held during an informal NATO defense ministerial meeting in Colorado Springs in October 2003.[12] According to reports of the meeting, a number of European defense ministers complained that the scenario did not mention the UN and that no background information was

---

[9] On diminishing European confidence and trust in U.S. foreign policy see: *Eurobaromètre 59*, Spring 2003.

[10] Barry R. Posen, "Command of the Commons: the Military Foundation of U.S. Hegemony," *International Security*, Summer 2003.

[11] See for example: Guillaume Parmentier, "Le débat interne sur le rôle des États-Unis dans le monde," *Questions Internationales*, September-October 2003, La Documentation française, Paris.

[12] Colorado Springs, USA, October 8-9, 2003.

provided regarding the political situation leading to the simulated crisis. As a result, many of them were dilatory during the scenario and indicated they could not commit forces unless such action was approved by their respective national parliaments.[13] In short, European reactions to this scenario underscored distrust regarding the Pentagon's approach to solving military crises outside NATO's traditional boundaries.

Reservations about U.S. foreign policy goals are now seriously affecting the role and place of NATO at the same time as adaptations launched at NATO's Prague summit in November 2002 are transforming the command structure of the Alliance and adjusting its military posture. Nevertheless, NATO has been pushed by Washington to base its own evolution on U.S. "transformation" efforts. Former SACLANT Admiral Forbes has underscored this view: "A transformational process akin to that which has been taking place in the United States is essential to modernize the Alliance's capabilities and ensure that they stay consistent with U.S. military thinking and development."[14]

As already mentioned, the problem is that these efforts at change and "Alliance transformation" no longer coincide with an automatically agreed vision of the international scene between the U.S. and many of its European allies, as during the Cold War. The more NATO is called upon by the U.S. to play an out of area role, the less political support it can count on, because of the new U.S. unilateralism. If the U.S. lesson from Kosovo is that the military imperative to speed up the tempo of military operations now needs to be translated, within an Alliance context, to a kind of delegation of power from the NAC (North Atlantic Council) to SAC-O (Supreme Allied Command-Operation) reporting only to the Secretary General of the organization to conduct military operation outside the boundaries of Article 6 of the Washington Treaty, ones run the risk of disillusion. It seems quite difficult to imagine that European countries committing forces in a distant theater of operations, where the political situation may be complex and where local military decision may impact on their own internal security, will easily relinquish the ultimate control of their forces to a commander in chief over whom they will have no

---

[13] See *TTU, Lettre Hebdomadaire d'Informations Stratégiques*, No. 467, October 16, 2003.

[14] See the interview with Admiral Forbes in *Nato Review*, Summer 2003

authority. French Defense Minister Alliot-Marie has been keen to reaffirm repeatedly that allied military operation have to be based on prior common definition of political objectives, which implies tight control by allied political leaders over the implementation of military actions.[15] Indeed, it is doubtful whether NATO could in fact operate effectively outside its traditional geographical limits, since U.S. and European views towards international disputes are increasingly at odds—see, for example, the Israeli-Palestinian conflict.

In addition to that contentious issue, NATO runs the risk of taking a new physiognomy strongly reminiscent of the "Holly Alliance" set up in post Napoleonic Europe, when the Allies were eager to maintain the new European status quo in using military forces if necessary. At the beginning of the 21st century, the United States may be willing, together with some allies, to use its position of clear military supremacy to extend, even by force, democracy and free markets into unwilling parts of the world, as exemplified by Iraq. In this context, the present pressure, exerted mainly in Washington, on NATO to no longer be constrained geographically by article 6 implicitly indicates a will to transform not only NATO's range but also its raison d'être. Its vocation is no longer confined to thwarting military aggression, its new purpose is to "defend those principles and values which constitute the bedrock of our open society."[16] This eminent task is so vague that indeed it authorizes every type of action and opens the possibility that the Alliance address every type of problem that could be seen as threatening those values. This represents a very disruptive evolution likely to produce potentially dramatic internal political fallout.

British writer Hugo Young's comment about his country's role in the Iraqi crisis and Prime Minister Tony Blair's attitude is relevant in this connection. Blair, Young notes,

"had made his commitment to Bush, stating among other extraordinary things that it was Britain's national task to prevent the U.S. being isolated...he could not contemplate breaking free of ties and rituals that began with Churchill, and that both Downing Street and the Ministry

---

[15] Michèle Alliot-Marie, French Defense Minister, Speech at the dinner of NATO's Chiefs of Staff, Cannes, France, September 9, 2003

[16] Anna Palacio, Spanish Defense Minister, Statement, NATO Ministerial Meting, Madrid, June 3, 2003.

of Defense—the Foreign Office is somewhat wiser—have cultivated, out of fear and expectations for decade. He was driven by something, which none of his predecessors....has succumbed to. Without exception they all kept their eyes on the British ball....For Blair, in his Bush-Iraq mode, this has been a lot more theoretical: the theory of preemptive intervention in a third country's affairs, for moral purposes, at the instigation of the power whose hyperdom he cannot resist. What does that mean? That we have ceased to be a sovereign nation."[17]

In a sense one may argue that the new alliance could become the armed branch of the transformation of the world economy through the process of globalization, acting much as the far older "Holy Alliance." Such a *gendarme*'s role for the new NATO presupposes, as already mentioned, that the geographical scope of the Alliance go worldwide. Here again there is paradox. As NATO, particularly after expanding to 25 members, becomes less and less the kind of military alliance it used to be, new tasks are imposed upon it. The NATO Response Force (NRF) will certainly not solve the problem. *De facto* constitution of *ad hoc* coalitions will represent the best solution.

ESDP and "Transformation"

The growing drift between the two sides of the Atlantic about international issues potentially is risky when it appears that the Europeans have greater difficulties to influence American foreign policy. Such drift is occurring, paradoxically, at the same time as NATO military capabilities have become increasingly dependant upon the U.S. war machine. Only four EU countries annually spend more than €20 billion on defense. Most of them spend less than €5 billion. This means that with the exception of the UK, Germany and France, most European countries have lost their capability to plan and conduct military operations beyond the upper tactical level, and that coalition operations will be conducted by unequal partners. This factor was taken into account by the U.S. *Joint Vision 2020*, which acknowledged that "the Joint Force will also be capable of planning and conducting dominant maneuver in cooperation with interagency and with multinational partners with varying levels of commitment and capability."

---

[17] "Under Blair, Britain has ceased to be a sovereign state," Hugo Youg, *The Guardian*, September 16, 2003.

Indeed, 18 countries of the 25 in the enlarged EU have military forces with manpower below 50,000 men. Most of them, with the exception of the United Kingdom with the PJHQ (Permanent Joint Headquarter) and France with the CPCO (*Centre de Planification et de Conduite des Opérations*) and in the near future Germany, are no longer able to prepare and execute military operations at the operational and strategic levels. They do not possess adequate intelligence and transmission systems nor a balanced system of forces to launch by themselves such operations. No EU countries, with the exception of Great Britain and France, have force projection capabilities to enter by force on some distant theater, a *sine qua non* condition to be lead nation for any type of EU military intervention as recently demonstrated at the occasion of the *Artemis* operation. In terms of force projection, Britain and France amount to about 50 per cent of the combat surface fleet of the 15 current EU members. Both have demonstrated the ability to project alone and sustain large amount of forces in Africa or in the Persian Gulf for combat operations.

Traditionally, each of the EU's three principal military powers— France, Germany, and Great Britain—have sought to cultivate bilateral cooperation with the U.S. in order to influence Washington's conduct of war within a coalition framework. The three countries are now coming to realize that only by achieving a convergence of their own views on military affairs will they have enough weight to influence Washington. This is due to a variety of factors, including major U.S. advances in military spending and capabilities; the difficulties experienced by UK armed forces when planning military operations with the U.S. for the recent war in Iraq;[18] mounting U.S. problems in Iraq following the war; and the growing realization that the EU eventually could possess adequate capabilities to plan and conduct military operations at the strategic and operational level. There is, of course, no clear consensus on this view within the three countries although they stand more on a convergence line than ever before. There is still considerable reluctance to overcome in the British and German ministries of defense, which explains in part why the Europeans will continue to move ahead slowly.[19]

---

[18] On the disappointment felt by the British see: Quentin Peel, "Talking Europe, Thinking Britain," *Financial Times*, September 25, 2003

[19] "European leaders at odds with ministers over EU defense plan", *Financial Times*, October 15, 2003

The last consideration leading some Europeans to be cautious about blindly following the U.S. "transformation" process is related to Washington's attitudes towards the EU. In the spring of 2003, when the EU was embroiled in a complex and delicate exercise to define a constitution, some hard liners in Washington launched an offensive against the EU aimed at its "disaggregation." The first shot were fired during the opening if the Iraqi crisis when the "Vilnius Ten"—a loose grouping of candidate countries for NATO membership—were cleverly manipulated by Bruce Jackson, former vice-president of Lockheed Martin and an informal adviser to the Bush Administration. Since that episode, skirmishes have been frequent, and have reached such intensity that the EU's High Commissioner for Foreign and Security Affairs, Javier Solana, were compelled to warn the U.S. not to succumb to the temptation to play the card of "disaggregating Europe."

The EU's agenda is to complete an overall European construction that gives the EU a say in world affairs: "We, the members of the European Council, are resolved that the European Union shall play its full role on the international stage."[20] In military affairs, this implies that the EU must acquire the capacities and the capabilities, at the strategic level, independently to assess a crisis and consider its potential military implications, to plan military operations if necessary and to execute such operations using European assets: "...we are convinced that the Council should have the ability to take decisions on the full range of conflict prevention and crisis management....This requires a capacity for autonomous action backed up by credible military capabilities and appropriate decision making bodies... the EU will need a capacity for analysis of situations, and a capability for relevant strategic planning."[21] This emphasis on autonomous action is a significant point of orientation guiding EU efforts to develop, over the medium-term, both appropriate political-military structures and military tools to fulfill the goals assigned to ESDP.

Accordingly, between 1999-2002, the EU set up relevant political-military structures to assess, decide, plan and implement military operations. Although these structures are in their infancy, they have

---

[20] European Council Declaration on Strengthening the Common European Policy on Security and Defence, Cologne European Council, June 3-4, 1999.

[21] Ibid. Since then, those objectives have been reiterated at various European Council meetings.

been tested by two EU military operations: *Concordia* and *Artemis*. *Concordia* is a EU military operation, drawing on NATO assets, launched after the U.N. Security Council agreed to the request of the President of the Former Yugoslav Republic of Macedonia to stabilize a volatile situation in the western part of his country. A small EU force (about 400 personnel) was dispatched under a command structure provided at the strategic level by NATO. This was made possible after the EU finally reached an agreement with NATO regarding the implementation of EU-led military operations drawing on NATO assets (basically U.S. assets). These EU-NATO arrangements, known in defense circles as the "Berlin Plus agreements," were adopted at the 2002 Prague summit. Political control and strategic direction for the operation were provided by the EU's Standing Political and Security Committee (PSC), whereas the commander of the operation at the strategic level was provided by NATO. An EU Operational Headquarters was set up at SHAPE (Supreme Headquarters Allied Powers in Europe) under the supervision of NATO's deputy SACEUR, who is a European. The command of the force in Macedonia was established in Skopje.

In the case of operation *Artemis*, the operation was fully controlled and managed by the Europeans. The EU launched the operation in the Democratic Republic of Congo (DRC) in accordance with UNSC Resolution 1484 of May 30, 2003 and the EU Council's Joint Action adopted on June 5, 2003. The operation, which involved about 2000 men deployed in Africa,[22] ended officially on September 1, 2003. The UN Resolution authorized the deployment of an interim emergency multinational force in Bunia to the security situation and to improve humanitarian conditions in Bunia. France acted as the "Framework Nation" for the operation. It used its new strategic command structure (the CPCO- *Centre de Planification et de Conduite des Operations*),[23] a part of which was "Europeanized" with the inclusion of about 30 officers from other EU countries to complement the 50 French officers assigned to set up the EU's headquarters. An operational EU headquarters was also established in Entebbe (Uganda) to directly command the operation.

---

[22] On this occasion, Swedish special forces were operationally deployed in Africa for the first time.

[23] The CPCO will be fully operational in 2006. Germany and Britain (PJHQ) each have an equivalent structure.

What Challenges Does U.S. Military "Transformation" Pose for Europeans?

The first challenge for Europeans is to remain able to cope with America's ongoing military-technical revolution. This means developing and building complex new weapon systems, particularly in the fields of intelligence, operational military planning and information dominance. To reach that capability Europeans will have to take on the difficult task of pulling together their disparate research and development resources in the context of low defense spending. As ESDP cooperation deepens, limits on national defense spending will probably lead towards "mutualisation" of forces and eventually to force specialization according to commonly defined doctrine and operational guidance.

European countries also need to confront the question of compatibility of their force posture with that of the U.S., either within NATO or within the framework of ESDP. If Washington is "transforming" part of its military forces, what shall be the European attitude? Should the Europeans, for the sake of interoperability, follow the U.S. lead when no single European nation has enough resources to develop a full "transformational" force? Would it be satisfactory to develop only "niche" capabilities in the U.S. "system of systems"? Can the EU adequately advance the role it wishes to play on the international scene if it remains capable only of providing forces, mainly on the ground, which in turn are dependent on intelligence and data flows processed by U.S. forces? Such a situation would be reminiscent of the status of colonial forces serving in British and French armies during the colonial period.

How should Europeans relate to U.S. "transformation" efforts? The answer has less to do with the future characteristic of armed conflict than with the political significance of military choices. Europe possesses enough know-how and experience regarding various types of military conflict, ranging from peace keeping operations to high intensity combat, as well as the high-tech know-how necessary to develop a military posture within ESDP that would be cooperable with U.S. forces but not codeterminous with U.S. force posture, and that would relate directly to the political and strategic needs of the EU.

Step by step, European defense is on the move. Either nationally or collectively the Europeans are gradually developing tools that will be of paramount importance to fulfill the goal of strategic autonomy. In the domain of intelligence satellites, for example, they will have about 15 reconnaissance satellites (including dual-use ones) in the next 5 years. In navigation systems the development of the Galileo satellite system will give a tremendous impetus to autonomous European capabilities in areas ranging from pure navigation to planning long-range strike. To quote the *Financial Times*: "the way to gain more autonomy from the U.S. without further worsening transatlantic ties lies in concrete measures."[24]

If the first ESDP challenge is reaching a political consensus to deepen European military integration, the second is reconciling the very wide variances in military manpower, defense budgets and capacities between different EU member states. Of course, each EU nation has an equal say in the development of European defense. But only a few EU countries are capable of planning and executing military operations at the strategic and operational level. This means that the primary responsibility to advance EU military capacity rests with the EU's three key military actors—France, Germany, and Great Britain.. They face three simultaneous tasks. The first is to continue to adapt and modernize their own military apparatus in order to maintain their capabilities to project forces and to plan military operations at the various level of warfare. Second, they have to begin "Europeanizing" their forces, due to the complexity and cost of modern weapons. Third, they have to maintain appropriate channels with their American ally in order to remain able to operate worldwide with U.S. forces. This last goal may be an important consequence of working together in the MIC. Cooperation in the MIC may also help to accelerate a full-fledged ESDP, co-operable with U.S. forces but tailored to accord with "European" political, cultural, historical, technological and doctrinal realities.

Conclusion

Development of a genuine European defense cannot avoid the traditional political difficulties related to the construction of a true European Union. Different views of the ultimate nature of the EU do not only derive from different interests; they are also directly linked to different historical experiences with the process of European integra-

---

[24] "Galileo gathers pace," *Financial Times*, September 22, 2003.

tion. Few countries have been part of this process for almost fiftyfive years, and some are not even full members of the Union. As mentioned by French president Jacques Chirac: "Europe…is not a freeway on which everyone can move fast. It is a steep and difficult mountain…some walk a bit faster, some more slowly because they are tired, others twist their ankles in a hole. But, we have never turned back."[25] This is the case in such domains as trade, economic policy, and monetary affairs. And now it is the case in defense.

For a certain period of time heterogeneity will prevail within the EU in the field of defense matters. That situation will almost certainly lead to the formation of an ESDP "pioneer group." The April 2003 Brussels meeting between Germany, France, Belgium and Luxembourg, which advanced the notion of an common strategic headquarters, open to other members of the EU, was a foretaste of that evolution.

Current limitations on Britain's strategic freedom of maneuver—the price of its special relationship with the U.S.—will delay London's full participation in this process, although British defense intellectuals are already considering what must be done to give birth to this inevitable process. British authorities now acknowledge that "structured cooperation," as outlined in the EU constitution draft, should be possible in defense." Structured cooperation" refers to the idea that, within the very complex set of policies developed in the EU, some countries may decide, on some issues, in this case defense, to develop aspects of cooperation that other members are unable or momentarily unwilling to advance. In a certain sense, on defense France, Germany and Britain are moving ahead, playing the role of an *avant-garde* left open to the others members to join. If, by example, Poland is among the natural eligible candidates, the state of its military apparatus and its excessive leaning towards U.S. positions in defense affairs makes almost impossible for Polish authorities to accept the meaning and the strategic implication of "structured defense" cooperation, i.e. the creation of a genuine and autonomous EU military policy.

Indeed, when meeting in September 2003, Gerhard Schröder, Jacques Chirac and Tony Blair agreed "The European Union should

---

[25] Jacques Chirac, interview with *The New York Times*, September 22, 2003.

be endowed with a joint capacity to plan and conduct operations without recourse to NATO resource and capabilities. Our goal remains to achieve such a planning and implementation capacity either by consensus with the 25 [members states] but also in a circle of interested partners."[26]

Such cooperation would enable those members of the EU who wanted to move ahead with defense initiatives to do so without waiting for the agreement of non-participants. This will open a new phase of European defense construction, following the initial cycle of activity between 1999 and 2003. Initially, only a few countries will take part in this new phase. But others will join sooner or later. This new cycle is not geared to producing a "war machine" directed against any country or alliance. It is the continuation of the European construction. In the process most EU member states will regain their lost capacity to think strategically, to understand a crisis strategically and if necessary to protect the collective interest of the EU with unsurpassed efficiency. This will create possibilities that the U.S. will never give to its allies, not even the closest. The creation of a European military pillar will greatly enhance the overall capacity of the Atlantic alliance. It can also be compatible with efforts to work closely with Washington on certain aspects of "transformation," notably in the doctrinal domain.

---

[26] Internal document approved at the Berlin meeting between Tony Blair, Jacques Chirac and Gerhard Schröder, September 20, 2003. See, Bertrand Benoit and Ben Hall, "Blair backs more EU defence co-operation," *Financial Times*, September 22, 2003.

Chapter 5

Transforming the German *Bundeswehr*—The Way Ahead

Manfred Engelhardt

Introduction

The current strategic environment poses challenges that go far beyond the territorial defense of Germany or the regional defense of Europe. The German government is being forced to reconsider the fundamentals of its security and defense policy. In the 21st century, global threats and risks affect all societies. Security cannot be "regionalized;" it must be advanced with a global perspective.

To some, this may seem obvious. But this global dynamic is generating dramatic changes in Germany's political agenda. These changes are comparable in their importance with those that occurred during the early days of the Federal Republic, including the creation of the Bundeswehr itself. They are transforming thinking about security in Germany today, particularly how to organize, structure and equip the Bundeswehr with instruments which are appropriate and effective to implement modern German defense policies.

During the early days of the Cold War, only foreign forces provided a security umbrella over Germany, which gave the German people a chance to reconstruct their country in a peaceful environment. Initially, the German "Basic Law"[1] did not include any defense policy provisions at all. Germany as a state did not even have a military. Therefore, creating the Bundeswehr and integrating the Federal Republic of Germany into the common defense of the West through NATO was a dramatic and radical change—a change of paradigms with far reaching implications for domestic politics as well as for the role of Germany in the international arena.

---

[1] The "Basic Law" of 1949 had been the provisional constitution of the western part of the divided Germany until unification in 1990, when subsequently it became the constitution of the unified Germany. Defense provisions were amended as part of the so-called "defense-constitution package" alongside the Paris Treaties/NATO-accession ratification process (1954-1955).

In subsequent decades the Bundeswehr experienced a continuous process of reform and modernization as it adapted to new standards, technology, doctrinal changes, and operational requirements in line with NATO's strategic and operational doctrines. The basic assumption, nevertheless, remained the same—participation in the common defense of German or NATO-partner territory. Though there were debates on an "extended security concept," a "broader understanding of security," or "common and comprehensive security," a more traditional meaning and understanding of security through military defense prevailed. Furthermore, NATO doctrine and the Alliance's military organizational and command framework supplanted any specific German national security strategy or the development of a particularly German national command and control authority and organization.

The dramatic change of the politico-strategic environment following the collapse of the communist system in Europe and the Soviet Union, together with the economic consequences of globalization and the socio-technological revolutions of the Information Age, all had an enormous impact on German policy. The varied challenges posed by the "New World Order"—which in fact was more whirling disorder—required radical changes, ranging from mindsets to military instruments. Taken together, these changes can be summarized under the term "transformation."

Transformation has become a term of art to describe the continuous process of reconsidering the ways and means how nations provide for security in a single, comprehensive and integrated policy. It has also become the buzzword to describe the military changes needed to implement new capabilities to match current and future challenges.

In short, transformation has become a political task and a military goal—a mission derived from a vision for using Information Age technologies, proven business practices and management procedures, and knowledge-based leadership in security and defense management.

It has become a standard term and military task, first and foremost for the U.S., but also for NATO as well as individual NATO allies such as Germany. The strategic requirements and the vision needed by the German Bundeswehr are the same as for other allies. [2] The main differences are more semantic[3] than substantive in nature.

The Generalinspekteur der Bundeswehr (German Chief of Defense) characterizes the current effort as a "comprehensive transformation"[4] which goes far beyond the notions of reform, modernization or adaptation. It is a new way to implement German security policy in the Information Age and to enable German military forces to remain powerful tools for the German government.[5] It is an across-the-board "way to think, train, exercise, and fight,"[6] and thereby shape the military of the future.

Initial Steps

It is also important to understand current debates over "transformation" in the context of German unification. One could say that the Bundeswehr has been engaged in a major transformation process since 1990.

This process started with the changing strategic environment accompanying the unification of Germany. The Bundeswehr was forced to radically reconsider its ways of doing military business. Changing mindsets is the most important part of any transformation process, and the German defense community, especially soldiers, had to rethink the role and purpose of the Bundeswehr in the new strategic setting. Forces had to be reorganized to cope with new challenges and new threats, but also with new opportunities offered by technol-

---

[2] "We will continue to keep the transformation of the Bundeswehr in line with the transformation of NATO and the security and defense policy orientation of the European Union." German Defense Minister Peter Struck, when introducing the Defense Budget 2003 to the German Parliament on December 4, 2002.

[3] "Transformation means different things to different people." Ian Roxborough, "From Revolution to Transformation. The State of the Field," *Joint Forces Quarterly*, No. 32, Autumn 2002, pp. 68-75: The official German defense policy documents refer to "Fundamental Reform of the Bundeswehr" as the German equivalent.

[4] Generalinspekteur der Bundeswehr, *Generalinspekteurbrief 01/2003*. Berlin, October 1, 2003

[5] On the far reaching notion of transformation, where "more than technological advances were involved" and which is "not synonymous with modernization," see also Roxborough, op. cit., pp. 68-69.

[6] Donald Rumsfeld, "Transforming the Military," *Foreign Affairs*, Vol. 81, Nov. 3, May/June 2002, p. 29.

ogy, new management procedures, and interoperability as the requirement for multinational operations.

The first step toward this transformation process began on the day
of German unification, October 3, 1990, when the Bundeswehr took
over responsibilities for manpower, materiel and property of the disbanded National People's Army of the deceased German Democratic
Republic.[7] Under the policy of "uniting not dividing," select former
members of the National People's Army were inducted as soldiers into
the Bundeswehr. On that day, eastern and western Germans began
serving side-by-side without any reservations due to the past. The policy was to integrate rather than to exclude—to overcome the division
between East and West as a key political goal. Today, the Bundeswehr
literally is the Bundeswehr-of-Unity with soldiers born and raised in
the East and soldiers born and raised in the West serving together in
almost every unit. The only obvious distinction is dialect—but this is
nothing new, since southern born Germans also speak differently than
northern born ones.

If one thinks in historic terms, and if one refers to other regions in
the world where similar situations exist—this process of "mentally first"
transforming the German military has been an outstanding success.[8]

This process was also accompanied by conceptual changes. The
Cold War strategic and operational mission of the Bundeswehr was
rendered obsolete. The need for the Bundeswehr itself remained as a
means to provide for security and stability, but in a very new context.
The notion that the post-Cold War "peace dividend" could also
include disbanding German military forces in general, as relicts of the
past, proved to be wrong. A new perception of reality began to dawn.

---

[7] On October 3, 1990, at midnight sharp, the German Democratic Republic (GDR—in
German: DDR) ceased to exist: the GDR joined the Federal Republic of Germany.
Associated with this accession came the disbanding of the National People's Army; the
armed forces of the GDR were not "integrated" but dissolved. On the political, social and
military issues of this unique endeavor, see Jörg Schönbohm, *Zwei Armeen und ein
Vaterland. Das Ende der Nationalen Volksarmee* (Two Armies and One Vaterland. The End of
the National People's Army). Berlin 1992

[8] The only distinction still existing between the "Ossis" i.e. East Germans and "Wessis" i.e.
West Germans in the Bundeswehr is an unequal payment structure resulting from regulations in the Unification Treaty, which governs all aspects of the political and social integration of the former GDR. Although payscales are gradually converging, this topic causes
concern and needs to be solved in the near future.

First, stability in central Europe does not mean peace on earth. Second, to preserve peace and stability at home in a globalizing world, Germany and its partners must be prepared either to export security and stability or face the alternative of importing instability and insecurity. Third, this means thinking globally and acting nationally to shoulder one's share of global responsibility.

In security terms, this means out with the old rules, in with the new. For the Bundeswehr, this means shifting the primary task from common defense of German or allied territory to participating in missions never even thought of, in areas never considered as a German area of responsibility. It means changing from a territorial defense force to deployable forces engaged in regional conflicts. It means defining a particularly German "politico-strategic interest," creating a national command and control authority outside the existing NATO-command structure, assuring communications and information through the echelons up to the ministerial level, and envisaging long-term, long-range deployment of personnel as the rule, not the exception.

These changes required a political reconception of the role and function of the military. The way was cleared by the German Constitutional Court's decision on July 12, 1994 that Bundeswehr deployments under the mandate of collective security institutions were both legitimate and legal under German constitutional law. This marked the birth of the new German security and defense policy.

The attack on the World Trade Towers and the Pentagon on September 11, 2001 was the last wake-up call that peace must be earned and defended, every day, against new threats and villains—and requires global commitments and engagement. This again would mean new concepts and doctrines, appropriate organizational and educational frameworks, equipment and infrastructure. It would mean, in short, a Bundeswehr capable and prepared of conducting new political missions and assisting in exporting security across the globe, in multinational settings, over extended periods of engagement.

The Present Situation

These changes did not occur overnight. This multifaceted transformation process takes time, costs money, and calls for new ways and means to make the Bundeswehr capable of these new tasks. Currently, the Bundeswehr is in the middle of the process: first steps taken, others not waged, further approaches not yet implemented.

On the other hand, the changes are stunning if one simply looks at current Bundeswehr operations. Today 7,500-10,000 German soldiers are permanently deployed and engaged in eight different missions on three continents.

Figure 1   German Troops in Operations as of November, 2003

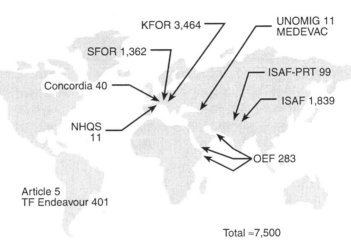

KFOR 3,464

UNOMIG 11
MEDEVAC

SFOR 1,362

Concordia 40

ISAF-PRT 99

ISAF 1,839

NHQS
11

OEF 283

Article 5
TF Endeavour 401

Total ≈7,500

courtesy of Ministry of Defense—Office of D/CHOD

About 100,000 service personnel have had "expeditionary experience" since 1998.[9] This is now largely accepted in German political life as normal.

Mission planning and operational command and control rest with a unified command headquarters—the Bundeswehr Operations Command, located in Potsdam. This is the only joint forces headquarters of the Bundeswehr, responsible for all missions and operations,

---

[9] Jürgen Bornemann, "Network Centric Capabilities—sicherheitspolitische Rahmenbedingungen und militärpolitische Implikationen," in Studiengesellschaft der DWT mbh., ed., *Network Centric Capabilities und der Transformationsprozess. Kompendium des Symposiums 4. September 2003.* (DWT: Bonn 20030, pp. 3-6. Brigadier General Bornemann serves as Deputy Assistant Chief of Staff, Federal Armed Forces Staff, for Military Policy and Arms Control, at the Ministry of Defense in Berlin.

subordinated and reporting directly to the Generalinspekteur (Chief of Defense).

This headquarters underpins the new role and function—and increased responsibility as well as authority—of the Generalinspekteur. As chairman of the "Operations Council," he coordinates, guides and controls the "operational Bundeswehr." This is a major change from the former distinct and distributed responsibilities of the Chiefs of the Services. This new role constitutes the Generalinspekteur not only as the first military advisor to the cabinet, but also as the operational head of the forces.

Implementation of a single national command and control organization has been accompanied by other changes. Just as "jointness" is considered to be a central goal for U.S. military transformation, "Streitkräftegemeinsamkeit" is a central goal for Bundeswehr transformation. This German version of "jointness" is not about the addition of capabilities as developed and maintained separately by the services, it is about the capability of the Bundeswehr as a whole and the specific contributions each service can provide to achieve overall capabilities.

German "jointness" is also about avoiding duplication. The Bundeswehr simply cannot afford to spend money it does not have to spend for things already available—it has more serious investment needs than duplication of capabilities. The first answer was to change the support echelon of the Bundeswehr by creating what forces in other nations call "joint or focused logistics." The Bundeswehr "Joint Support Service" now provides joint logistics and communications for all the services. Additionally, a centralized medical service supports all forces' services.

Logistical and medical support for an army unit operating in Bosnia, for example, will now be provided by the Joint Support Service and the Centralized Medical Service, rather than be a natural part of the unit itself. These support elements can be better provided and maintained by the central organizations, due to the capabilities required in a specific area of commitment, than by multiple and various single-service support echelons employed in a fragmented setting. This change is not only an organizational alteration imposed by scarce resources, it is emblematic of a thorough transformation in the concept and conduct of military business. It is about improving the capabilities of the Bundeswehr as a whole.

This new way of thinking and acting goes further, reaching into the educational organization and infrastructure of the military. Instead of separated and independent single-service schools, joint schools will serve all services. Instead of fragmented services responsibility for strategic intelligence and reconnaissance, there is one Bundeswehr responsibility for military intelligence within the Ministry of Defense and its Joint Services Staff organization, with a joint Intelligence Office, and there is one Bundeswehr Strategic Reconnaissance Command. The Bundeswehr is also further developing the "jointness program" in the curricula for career soldier education, especially at the Command and General Staff Academy, the Führungsakademie.

In addition, all Bundeswehr bases are under scrutiny: The "Departmental Concept for Basing," as approved on February 16, 2001, calls for downsizing the total number of military bases and shifting from the concept of "balanced basing" throughout Germany. Given the new security environment and new operational guidelines, there is no need for basing premised on geographic balance throughout the country.

Moreover, the civilian side of the Bundeswehr is also in the process of realignment—Bundeswehr civilian manpower is being trimmed to 145,000 personnel and refocused on core military functions, while many other administrative functions are being outsourced to civil contractors.[10]

This new relationship with industry calls for new rules and regulations, and new administrative ways to handle the procurement process. A shorter and improved arms procurement cycle has been introduced through a new process entitled "CPM 2001"—the acronym standing for "Customer, Product, Management."

---

[10] This is an old issue in the public, parliamentary, and military debate on the distinction of these functions following provisions and interpretations of Basic Law Article 87a on the military and Article 87b on the Federal Administration within the Ministry of Defense. Following this separation of responsibilities, the civil sector of the Bundeswehr (arms procurement, information management, administration, legal and personnel branches) is not governed by the Generalinspekteur but reports to one State Secretary.

New missions, limited resources, and continuous downsizing following unification together demand a new understanding of the basic needs and operational requirements of this "Bundeswehr on Operations." The Bundeswehr has defined six areas or categories of capabilities essential for new missions: command and control; intelligence collection and reconnaissance; mobility; effective engagement; support and sustainability, and survivability and protection.

Within this framework key deficiencies have been identified, and priority has been given to improving capabilities in such areas as strategic deployment, global reconnaissance, and interoperable command and control and communication systems.

Critical Reappraisal

Transformation has considerable momentum. But these innovations continue to compete with the traditional organization, structure and force composition of the old Cold War Bundeswehr.

Significant parts of the budget still go to maintenance and operational costs, notably high personnel costs, rather than to necessary investment, research and development, or acquisition of innovative equipment. Furthermore, budget restrictions and limitations have impaired the Bundeswehr's capability to restructure and modernize adequately. The annual defense budget has been frozen at €24.25 billion[11] and will be increased by an additional €1 billion only in Fiscal Year 2007.

This imbalance between political and military missions, capabilities, structure, organization, and concepts, on the one hand, and available resources on the other, forced a critical reappraisal in 2003. New "Defense Policy Guidelines" for the Bundeswehr were issued by the German Minister of Defense on May 21, 2003, to replace decade-old ministerial guidance.[12]

---

[11] NATO's published defense appropriations and budget figures are different because of different criteria: according to NATO criteria, the German defense budget is about $30+ billion. Due to general savings and cuts, the actual 2004 defense budget is €23.8 billion.

[12] Bundesministerium der Verteidigung (Ministry of Defense), *Verteidigungspolitische Richtlinien*(Defense Policy Guidelines). Berlin 21.05.2003—English version available at http://suchc101.infosys.svc

These new defense guidelines radically replace traditional thinking about direct defense of German territory with the view that German security and defense has no limits in geographic terms.[13] As the Minister of Defense has said, threats to German security are more likely to come from outside Germany or the European region than from the Fulda Gap—which means that "German security will also be defended at the Hindu Kush," to use Minister Struck's often cited phrase. Consequently, there can be no geographic limitation on the Bundeswehr's area of operations: global deployment and engagement are to be regarded as normal. [14] These missions require a comprehensive, capability-oriented approach integrating all the armed services and organizational areas.[15]

This does not mean that "homeland territorial defense" is to be denied or neglected, but it can be provided with reconstitution provisions, because of the political and militarily usable warning and preparation time. Furthermore, greater importance must be given to inter-governmental cooperation and inter-agency coordination to assure that the rules and regulations separating authority for Germany's internal and external security do not prohibit effective response to new threats that do not respect such divisions of authority.

This understanding of comprehensive security takes political, economic, ecological, social and cultural conditions and developments into account,[16] and leads to three essential factors determining German defense policy. The first is multinationality, i.e. multinational integration of the Bundeswehr into the framework of German foreign policy, which is focused on European integration, transatlantic partnership, and global responsibility. The second factor is the changed operational spectrum of the Bundeswehr and the increased number of international operations. The third factor is that of available resources.[17]

---

[13] Manfred Engelhardt, "Neuausrichtung der Bundeswehr," in *Network Centric Capabilities*, op. cit., pp. 7-14.

[14] Bornemann, op. cit., p.5.

[15] *Defense Policy Guidelines*, op. cit., para 14.

[16] *Defense Policy Guidelines*, op. cit., para 36.

[17] *Defense Policy Guidelines*, op. cit., para 41.

To meet these challenges, all current parameters for the number and dimension of potential operations[18]—as well as equipment, structures, force size and composition—were scrutinized. Initial decisions in 2003 were directed at army, air force and naval assets and components, and each service was forced to abandon capabilities deemed no longer essential by 2005. The Army is downsizing its central combat capability, provided by its powerful tank force, and shifting to a mix of heavy, middle and light forces, limiting the armor fleet to somewhat more than 800 vehicles. Orders for the new TIGER support helicopter dropped from 110 to 80. The Air Force is disbanding the HAWK and ROLAND anti-aircraft missile components, and is to decommission two fighter-bomber wing-equivalents of about 90 TORNADO-aircraft. The Navy is disbanding the Naval Air Wing 2 and turning over its TORNADO-aircraft to the Air Force, which will assume responsibility for sea-strike capabilities. The Navy is also decommissioning 10 Fast Patrol-Boats class 143. All these tremendous cuts are to be accomplished by the end of 2005.[19]

Alongside these tasks, Defense Minister Struck ordered the Generalinspekteur to assess all equipment and procurement options and planning with a view to identifying further resources to enable the Bundeswehr to concentrate on the essentials. He was tasked to submit a proposal for a better force structure—to bridge the widening gap between expectations and requirements on the one hand, and the reality of limited resources on the other. This tasking recognized the obvious: The Bundeswehr is stretched to its limits. Obligations and commitments exceed existing capabilities, leeway for future-oriented investment and innovative acquisition is not available, restrictions are imposed on day-to-day operations, and basing costs exceed operational requirements. Together, these constraints are endangering the Bundeswehr's operational capabilities.

In short, Defense Minister Struck called for an operational plan to transform the Bundeswehr to meet the challenges of the future.[20]On October 1, 2003 the Minister issued the "Guidance for

---

[18] See *Defense Policy Guidelines*, op. cit., para 66.

[19] See Engelhardt, op. cit., p. 13.

[20] Defense Minister Peter Struck, Lecture at the Sicherheitspolitisches Forum NRW, Friedrich-Ebert-Stiftung. Bonn September 24, 2003.

the Further Development of the Bundeswehr"[21] and operational steps forward were elaborated by the Generalinspekteur, General Schneiderhan.[22] Together, these documents comprise what may be called the "Bundeswehr Transformation Roadmap."

The Future

The "Transformation Roadmap" is based upon the "Defense Policy Guidelines" of May 21, 2003, but calls for a greater understanding of basic requirements and needs. Very few fundamentals remain untouched. Almost everything is under revision: concepts, organization and structure, materiel and equipment, training and leadership education, infrastructure and basing.[23]

The transformation roadmap has three basic premises. First, the Bundeswehr must face the challenges of accelerating globalization, which in turn means being prepared for new forms and means of asymmetric warfare. Second, the challenges and opportunities offered by the Information Age, with real-time information available almost anywhere in the world, will have a greater impact on command and control of military forces. Third, multinationality—within the Alliance, in the EU, or in ad-hoc-coalitions—is the general rule for Bundeswehr operations. As a matter of principle, only "rescue and evacuation operations will be conducted as a national responsibility."[24]

---

[21] Bundesministerium der Verteidigung, *Weisung für die Weiterentwicklung der Bundeswehr* (Guidance for the Further Development of the Bundeswehr). Berlin, October 1, 2003— Except for the front page, the Guidance is classified "VS-Nur für den Dienstgebrauch/Restricted." The content of this "Guidance" was made public in detail by the Minister of Defense at his press conference on October 2, 2003.

[22] Generalinspekteur der Bundeswehr, *Generalinspekteurbrief 01/2003*, Berlin, October 1, 2003.

[23] The following argumentation follows lectures given by Major General H.-H. Dieter, Deputy Chief of Staff, Joint Support Services, and Acting Director, Armed Forces Staff, Ministry of Defense, Bonn: "Führung von Streitkräften im 21. Jahrhundert," and by Brigadier General Langheld, Assistant Chief of Staff and Head, Planning Division, Armed Forces Staff, Ministry of Defense, Bonn: "Planungen zur Verbesserung der Führungsfähigkeit," DWT-Forum on Führung, Führungsfähigkeit, Führungsunterstützung. Bonn-Bad Godesberg, October 8-9, 2003. Both lectures strongly rely upon the latest "Guidance" of the Minister of Defense. BG Langheld refers explicitly to this document. The lectures will be published soon.

[24] *Defense Policy Guidelines*, op. cit., para 81.

Figure 2   Transformation of German Defense Policy

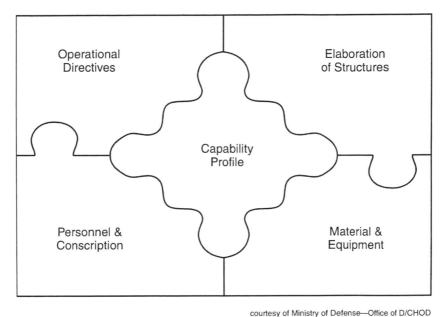

Operational
Directives

Elaboration
of Structures

Capability
Profile

Personnel &
Conscription

Material &
Equipment

courtesy of Ministry of Defense—Office of D/CHOD

These varied operational demands necessitate the unrestricted application of combinedness and jointness in thinking and acting. The Bundeswehr's overall capability therefore takes priority over the capabilities of the individual services.[25]

Three "constants" remain cornerstones for the new orientation, and are not subject to reassessment or reorientation. These are the international commitments of the Bundeswehr, the basic compulsory service of nine months duration (only to be modified in the manner of its implementation), and the general approach to greater cost-efficiency and cooperation with industry.

The capabilities' profile of the Bundeswehr as a whole is being subjected to high-priority review. The Bundeswehr must be capable of conducting operations over the whole mission spectrum. Only the intensity and duration of each operation within this spectrum are to be considered limiting factors for a military commitment following the political decision for engagement. Whether in the end the Bundeswehr itself

---

[25] *Defense Policy Guidelines,* op. cit., para 89.

must possess each and every capability, or whether certain capabilities might be best utilized through international cooperation, will become an issue especially within enhanced and increased European cooperation as part of the EU's European Security and Defense Policy (ESDP).

A second area of high priority is adapting operational determinants and mission profiles to financial reality. The entire Bundeswehr cannot be reorganized, restructured, reequipped, retrained and prepared to take part in any conceivable operation—this is beyond any reasonable financial funding. Instead, there will be gradually differentiated profiles for specific forces in accordance with paramount profiles at each level of engagement. Particular priority will be given to "spearhead" or Intervention Forces capable for all kind of operations (including their integration into the NATO Response Force or as part of the EU's Rapid Reaction Forces). This category of state-of-the-art, high readiness forces will comprise of about 35,000 soldiers. A second tier of "Bundeswehr on Operations" forces will be Stabilization Forces of about 70,000 personnel, trained and equipped for lower-level yet longer-duration engagements.

These forces will be supplemented by Support Forces providing also for basic homeland requirements, training facilities and further needs; and a Reserve component under the Generalinspekteur's discretion, which together will form the future backbone of the transformed Bundeswehr.

In sum, only mission-oriented functions and activities will survive the assessment and re-evaluation process—all other legacy functions, structures, and institutions will have to go.

This evaluation process includes implementation of basic compulsory service within the Bundeswehr. Draftees will remain a central component of the Bundeswehr, in part because about one third of the candidates for non-commissioned officer billets are recruited from the pool of soldiers serving the basic service time of nine months; but more importantly because the larger draft pool also produces volunteers for longer-term compulsory service, who are then able to serve as short-term enlisted personnel in deployment operations.[26]

---

[26] German Law allows for conscripts to serve for extended periods—up to 23 months—without loosing the privileges granted under the Compulsory Service Act; these soldiers are paid regular "volunteers wages" during that time.

This newly structured and mission-oriented capabilities profile demands commensurate adaptations of materiel and equipment planning. This is one of the most challenging tasks for the Generalinspekteur because of existing treaties and procurement programs, which have to be maintained for legal reasons, but which also claim key budgetary resources for fixed time periods.

To make ends meet, this transformation agenda calls for a trim Bundeswehr with reduced forces. By the end of 2010 the Bundeswehr will consist of 250,000 military personnel (down from the current size of about 282,000) and 75,000 civil servants (i.e. almost half the size of the current 145,000).[27]

One consequence of this smaller force will be a revision of the basing concept, following military and functional criteria rather than geographic balance. There will be more base closures, and troops will be concentrated in fewer garrisons.[28]

These challenges are focused on one single politico-military issue: using transformation to preserve the relevance of the Bundeswehr as a political instrument for force projection.[29]

The "Transformation Roadmap," as laid out in the two guiding documents mentioned above, is forcing the German strategic community, and especially the military, to rethink security, reorganize the Defense Ministry, restructure forces, reconsider warfighting through new concepts, and experiment with new procedures—in short, to "translate" transformation into operational reality.

At the center of this process is the need to be interoperable with allied and partner forces. This requires, inter alia, equal standards in central operational concepts—in other words, being capable of participating in networked military operations as the dominant operational concept of our partner nations. The full consequences of this new prerequisite for operational readiness are still being assessed—but the way has been cleared. The new "Concept of the Bundeswehr"—the

---

[27] Press conference of the Federal Minister of Defense, Dr. Peter Struck, on "Neue Aufgaben—neuer Kurs" (New tasks—new course), Berlin, October 2, 2003.

[28] Langheld, op. cit.

[29] Gerhard Schulz, "Multinational Joint Concept Development & Experimentation. Perspektiven fuer die Bundeswehr," in *Network Centric Capabilities* op. cit., pp. 15-22.

military doctrinal guidance for all planning, organizational and managerial behavior, for force structuring and training, for procurement decisions and acquisition—puts "networking" and "networked operations" in the center.

Does this mean that all military assets will be equally capable of participating in "networked operations?" Or, put another way, can we afford to make "networked operations" the single operational standard of all units? The simple answer is no—budget restraints alone prohibit this kind of spending. A prioritized approach is necessary. This means "active echelon" or intervention forces for international commitments are to be equipped "state-of-the-art," fully interoperable and able to participate in international network-enabled and oriented missions. All other forces are to be enhanced in a gradually differentiated manner with regard to their multinational commitments.

This means differentiating standards for different forces, which offers important implications for future force planning. The forthcoming "Concept of the Bundeswehr" will pay particular attention to such technological implications as adequate command and control equipment, organizational and informational management requirements, and the need to link assets and commands over "organizational boundaries."

These issues received first priority by the Generalinspekteur when addressing "Networked Operations" as the central category fundamental to the reassessment and realignment of all military capabilities.[30] But it is important to note that gradual differentiation of the forces can also mean preserving existing capabilities and equipment if they are compatible with the new central operational concept.[31]

The new concept of Networked Operational Capabilities is not only about "linking" those central categories of capabilities; it is also about creating a comprehensive "informational infrastructure," including sensors, decision makers, and effectors. It is about a comprehensive new dimension of interoperable planning, effects-oriented

---

[30] Langheld, op. cit.

[31] Furthermore, the need to link command and control, intelligence and reconnaissance, and "effects on target" had already been recognized as an underlying concept when the initial capabilities categories were being defined. See Langheld, op. cit.

decision making, and operations, "within a single informational framework." To achieve this networked operational capability for a single set of forces that is able to contribute to international efforts, only "common capabilities" are important. In short, the key is coherent jointness of the "single force." This calls for strengthening the role, function, and authority of the Chief of Defense, and for a new organizational framework and new "bylaws" for the Ministry of Defense and the way it acts. The new functional documents, which replace the outdated organizational guidelines of the Bundeswehr's early years, should move the military in this direction.[32]

These documents will have a tremendous impact on organizational improvements, too—affecting both the way the Ministry of Defense is run and how comprehensive planning for the future is organized and conducted. In this regard, common information and planning tools with shared databases is essential. Implementation and enhanced introduction of the "Standard Application Software Product Family—SASPF," based upon SAP R/3 software and associated programs, and the HERKULES-project as a common IT-backbone for the whole Bundeswehr, is of central importance.[33]

Restructuring and gradual differentiation of forces will determined priorities for procurement and acquisition, since not all Bundeswehr units will be equipped the same way and with the same hi-tech weaponry. The material status of a certain unit will depend on its force category, its mission determinants, and whether the specific equipment is affordable within given budget limits.

These decisions regarding structures, status and equipment obviously affect the training of troops. Training and education will be changed in accordance with these new force structures and requirements. Leadership education in particular will be changed. Skills cannot and will not be replaced by "self-synchronizing machines," by technology, or by micromanagement by superiors. In fact, in a networked environment the opposite is necessary; the leading principle of

---

[32] See Press conference of the Federal Minister of Defense, op cit., on the replacement of the so-called "Blankeneser Erlass," which regulates the responsibilities of the services' Chiefs of Staff and the role and function of the Generalinspekteur, and on revised "By-Laws" for intra-ministerial procedures by the end of 2003.

[33] See Press conference of the Federal Minister of Defense, op. cit.

"Auftragstaktik," or mission-oriented performance —the ability to alter one's course of action in response to changing battlefield awareness—will become even more important. [34]

To improve the Bundeswehr in this directed way, new concepts have to be developed, tested, evaluated and assessed before decisions will be made for implementation. The Concept Development and Experimentation (CD&E) process introduced initially by the U.S. armed forces, followed by partners within the Multinational Interoperability Council, and finally NATO, is a useful way to integrate new ideas, visions, concepts, management practices, business procedures, decision making processes, information- sharing and knowledge-building strategies, and innovations in every technological field. The creation of NATO's Supreme Allied Command Transformation, with CD&E as a key mission to enhance the capabilities of the Alliance and its members, and the close cooperation of this strategic command with U.S. Joint Forces Command, the U.S. "agent for transformation," underscores the importance of this endeavor.

Germany has been a member of the Multinational Interoperability Council (MIC) since 1999 and is actively engaged in this new range of transformation activities. Bundeswehr representatives chair MIC committees focused on enhancing interoperability standards and are actively engaged at the so-called "partner level" in CD&E-processes.[35] A national structure to facilitate German participation in CD&E processes is now being established within the Bundeswehr Center for Analyses and Studies. [36] Inter-agency cooperation, inter-service coop-

---

[34] Ralph Thiele, "Network Centric Capabilities und die Bedeutung des Transformationsprozesses für die Weiterentwicklung der Führungsinerstützung,"DWT-Forum on Führung, Führungsfähigkeit, Führungsunterstützung, Bonn-Bad Godesberg, 8-9 October 2003

[35] The Bundeswehr will keep its "partner status" as the appropriate level of engagement to ensure full information of results and ongoing experiments and to have the chance to participate actively with its own contributions in this process. This decision was reached at a meeting of the Militärischer Führungsrat on March 13, 2003. The Bundeswehr took part in the Limited Objective Experiment (LOE) 01 (2001) to evaluate new decision making procedures; in LOE 02 (2003) to test and assess forms of distributed information sharing with different procedures of the participating nations; and is part of the renamed Multinational Experiment (MNE) 03, to be conducted in 2004, with emphasis on Effects Based Planning procedures.

[36] The "Concept for the German Participation in CD&E-Processes" is the fundamental document providing a national organizational framework for CD&E activities. The concept received the Minister of Defense's endorsement on October 16, 2003. Central ele-

eration, cooperation with "outside agents" such as industry, universities and research institutes, and close coordination with partner institutions are further institutionalized procedures. With this CD&E-organization, the Bundeswehr will be able to fully participate in multinational and NATO-CD&E procedures as part of the transformation process—to quickly test, evaluate, and develop improvements for the forces to meet the challenges of the future.

Transforming the Bundeswehr—The Way Ahead

The new direction is clear: The new Bundeswehr must prepare consequently for probable mission engagements—with a global perspective. The core issues are conflict prevention and crisis management (including combating international terrorism), support of Alliance partners, and the protection of Germany, with rescue and evacuation as well as assistance operations to be further missions. To prepare the Bundeswehr for these missions, higher readiness, sustainable forces are required that are capable of being deployed quickly and effectively together with forces of other nations. Planning for these capabilities must be balanced by financial possibilities.

With this general commitment in mind, the Federal Minister of Defense publicly announced the Bundeswehr's transformation roadmap, entitled "Milestones for the New Direction," at a press conference on January 13, 2004.[37] Specifically, Minister Struck outlined six milestones for the transformation of the Bundeswehr.

ments within this structure—which at the end will comprise of 70 to 80 personnel—are the Concept Development branch, with two officers permanently detached to serve within the MNJCD&E-branch of USJFCOM; the Experiment Development branch collocated with the Operations Research Department of the Center for Analyses and Studies in Ottobrunn near Munich and in close working relationship with industrial capacities on Modeling and Simulation; the Experimental Laboratory with additional elements associated as a Standing Joint Forces Headquarters (SJFHQ)-nucleus, collocated with the (Joint) Bundeswehr Operations Command in Potsdam, and a System-of-Systems-Analysis-Cell co-located with the Bundeswehr Intelligence Office; and an Evaluation and Assessment Team, closely working with the Development offices/branches of the services and other organizational elements of the Bundeswehr, like the Information Technology Office, or the Arms Procurement Office. See Gerhard Schulz, op. cit.; Ralph Thiele, "Sachstand der deutschen Beteiligung an US Multinational Joint Transformation," in *Network Centric Capabilities*, op. cit., pp.33-40; Langheld, op. cit.

[37] The following remarks reflect the "Ausführungen des Bundesministers der Verteidigung, Dr. Peter Struck, anlässlich der Pressekonferenz am 13. Januar 2004 zur Konzeption und Weiterentwicklung der Bundeswehr," http://www.infosys.svc/C1256A4200206A74 January 14, 2004 (Statements by the Federal Minister of Defense Dr. Peter Struck at the press conference, 13 January 2004, on the Concept and Further Development of the Bundeswehr)

1. Capabilities. To conduct Bundeswehr operations in an enlarged and extended geographical area, as part of multinational operations within the full spectrum of operations, six intertwined categories of capabilities are essential for the Bundeswehr:

- Command and Control
- Intelligence Collection and Reconnaissance
- Mobility
- Effective Engagement
- Support and Sustainability
- Survivability and Protection

An internal review of Bundeswehr capabilities led Minister Struck to prioritize efforts that would develop greater capabilities in such areas as strategic mobility, global reconnaissance, effective and interoperable command and control systems, and missile defense. Force protection will be a necessity, given the enhanced operational requirements. This, in turn, calls for an unrestricted joint understanding in thinking and acting to achieve success in mission preparation and execution. Partial capabilities could be disbanded if they could be provided by other forces—an issue worthy of further consideration within NATO and the EU.

2. Operational Prerequisities. Meeting Germany's international commitments within the framework of the UN, NATO, EU, and the OSCE have been Bundeswehr tasks since the early 1990s. Adequate forces will be required not only for nation-building operations, but also for enforcement operations in a hostile environment. Such operations call for a sufficient, all-services enforcement contingent, capable of executing high intensity operations in a multinational setting. This requires networked operational capabilities based on the most up-to-date information technology.

Furthermore, German commitments have to be considered:

- permanent participation in NATO's Reaction Force (NRF), including pre- and post-phase and readiness components, calls for about 15,000 soldiers;
- the German contribution to the European Headline Goal is about 18,000 soldiers;

- within the UN Standby Arrangement System, Germany has declared a readiness component of up to 1,000 soldiers;

- some 1,000 soldiers will be maintained for evacuation operations under national responsibility.

All these forces will be provided from a single set of 35,000 highly trained forces, equipped to the highest standards and capable of networked operations in multinational missions. In addition to these forces, the Bundeswehr has to maintain adequate capabilities to provide for the protection of German territory and to assist in cases of emergencies. These forces are not deployed and therefore are available in Germany, but if necessary they could form the core of reconstitution measures.

3. Force categories.

- Intervention forces of about 35,000 personnel will be designated for high intensity multinational operations, as mentioned above.

- Stabilization forces will cover operations within the spectrum of peace stability missions. Though operating within scenarios of lower or medium intensity (but of extended duration), these joint forces must also be capable of engaging in hostile actions, with a heavy core and about 70,000 personnel, of which about 14,000 will be capable of being deployed permanently in up to five different missions.

- Support forces will comprise about 135,000 personnel, to enable engaged forces to accomplish their tasks as well to maintain the homeland base. Some of the approximately 75,000 civil servants of the Bundeswehr will be assigned as functional elements of the support forces.

This new system of force categories consequently calls for a new structuring of the organizational branches of the military—and for further downsizing of Bundeswehr personnel by another 35,000 military and another 10,000 civil billets.

4. Basing realignment. New structures, changing personnel levels, and greater demands for efficiency call for shrinking and realigning Bundeswehr bases. The initial basing concept of 2001 called for 505 bases to be maintained. The new Bundeswehr concept will force 100 further closures, with locations to be decided by end of 2004.

5. Matériel and Equipment. Procurement decisions will now reflect the requirements of likely future missions, rather than being based on prior decisions made in the context of defining territorial defense as the prime task of the Bundeswehr. The entire procurement process is under scrutiny, and is leading to severe cuts and a reorientation of further armaments plans. For example, a joint command and control/informations system is of foremost importance to enable networked operational capabilities, and appropriations procedures to support such a system are starting this year. Joint information collection and reconnaissance capabilities will also be developed, including the purchase of Maritime Patrol Aircraft MPA 3C ORION from the Netherlands and the German participation in NATO's Airborne Ground Surveillance System AGS.

Each service will also be affected by further procurement systems, which will be oriented to armored transport vehicles instead of unarmored trucks; the new main combat system of the armored infantry, PUMA, or the helicopters TIGER or NH90d; further 212-A class submarines; the "new frigate class 125" project; and 180 new Eurofighter aircraft. Each of these projects requires further assessment, including industrial participation. Further fine tuning of matériel and equipment and procurement policy will occur over the coming months and shall result in savings of about €26 billion. This shall provide leeway for distinct investments, starting in 2012, to equip adequately the "mission-engaged Bundeswehr."

6. Continuation of Compulsory Service. As mentioned in the "Defense Policy Guidelines," the basic service of nine months duration will be modified in its implementation. Conscripts remain essential to maintain the homeland basis of the Bundeswehr. They are also essential to the Bundeswehr's international commitments. Part of the forces committed to international operations are comprised of approximately 25,000 "conscripts serving voluntarily extended tours" of up to 23 months. Conscript skills and knowledge remain important to the Bundeswehr, but continuation of compulsory service remains a matter of broad political debate in Germany. The future structure of the Bundeswehr is being developed with this in mind. Should a political decision be taken against the draft after 2006, for instance, it would not result in a totally new reform of the Bundeswehr. Such a decision, however, would result in an additional 30-40,000 billets for voluntary personnel, resulting in huge additional funding for the Bundeswehr to accomplish the missions as outlined above.[38]

The six milestones on this transformation roadmap reflect the clear intention to shape the Bundeswehr of the 21st century in accordance with new mission requirements, requisite capabilities, structures, matériel and equipment, and basing concepts, within the bounds of Germany's financial possibilities.

Conclusion

Transformation of the Bundeswehr is not only about modernization or adaptation to changed conditions. It is about enabling the Bundeswehr to serve effectively as a vital instrument of the foreign and security policy of the Federal Republic of Germany—under a totally different and ever changing international environment with new and ever-changing threats and risks. It is about enabling the Bundeswehr to be flexible enough to improve capabilities quickly. This calls for flexibility, speed, and commitment. It calls for multinationality, interoperability, and the capacity to engage in networked operations, with jointness and combinedness as the leading organizational framework. It calls for information superiority and rapid, decisive operations. In sum, it calls for a different understanding of the task and mission of the Bundeswehr, and new ways to implement new means. It calls for the transformation of the Bundeswehr to be prepared to meet the challenges of the times ahead. There is no reasonable alternative to Bundeswehr transformation. Transformation is at the top of the German agenda too.[39]

---

[38] Statement of Minister Struck during the press conference answering questions—see: Frank Bötel, "Text: Pressekonferenz des Verteidigungsministers zur Weiterentwicklung der Bundeswehr—Wegmarken für den neuen Kurs—Berlin 13 Jan 2004," intr@net aktuell

[39] Bornemann, op. cit., p. 3.

Chapter 6

The Implications for Force Transformation: The Small Country Perspective

Rob de Wijk

Force restructuring encompasses force reduction, transition, modernization and transformation of armed forces; each has important financial, organizational and doctrinal consequences. It is an ongoing process and an enormous challenge for small countries. Because small countries possess limited budgets and small defense bureaucracies, their capacity to restructure is limited. They will find it hard, if not impossible, to restructure their forces in a comprehensive way. Difficult choices must be made. Priorities must be set.

This chapter offers an approach to force restructuring from the perspective of the small NATO member states. It argues that if those countries are to make credible contributions to multinational coalitions of the willing and able, they have no choice but to develop a more focused tool box, specialize in niche capabilities and contemplate pooling scarce assets and capabilities. However, if small countries no longer possess a broad range of military capabilities, but instead focus on limited, complementary capabilities, an unprecedented degree of defense integration is required. This, in turn, demands true partnership between NATO and the European Union's European Security and Defense Policy (ESDP). To make that happen, the major powers must work towards genuine transatlantic partnership and have no choice but to develop NATO and the EU as complementary and mutually reinforcing institutions.

The Concept of Restructuring

Force reduction is the first element of force restructuring. It logically emerged from the security situation after the end of the Cold War. There no longer is a need for large active and reserve forces that cannot be deployed abroad. Force reduction was relatively easy and allowed dramatic budget cuts. It was accompanied by a transition from conscripts to active, professional armed forces. Many NATO members decided to give up conscription, because for political reasons only professional soldiers could be sent abroad for combat missions. Because à professional armed force is more expensive, however, dramatic cuts in the size of armed forces were unavoidable. During the 1990s most NATO members reduced their armed forces by 25 to 50 per cent.

Disproportional cuts in the size of the armed forces were needed to relieve money for force modernization, the next element of force restructuring. Modernization basically has to do with replacing obsolete assets with new ones. It is a gradual process and distinct from force transformation, which concerns adapting armed forces to new methods of warfare. Modernization is evolutionary; transformation is revolutionary. In transformation, technology drives doctrine.

In the United States Network Centric Warfare (NCW), including Effects Based Operations as its critical enabler, has become the focus of transformation. Transformation requires new training, education, and command and control systems to allow operations in a 'netted' environment. It also requires short term investments, especially in software. The result of force transformation is armed forces capable of using innovative doctrines for new methods of warfare. Of all elements of force restructuring, transformation is the least understood and has perhaps the most unforeseen implications.

Most European NATO members tend to focus on reduction and transition. Some have funds for modernization, but most lack the money for transformation. The latter, however, is necessary because it holds the promise that military operations can be carried out quickly and decisively with limited risks to friendly forces and acceptable levels of collateral damage. Moreover, transformed military forces could conduct operations with fewer troops to achieve the objective. Without transformation, interoperability will be jeopardized as well. In sum, without transformation, a nation will no longer be able to contribute to international coalitions of the willing and able. Most importantly, a nation will not be able to turn its armed forces into a usable instrument of foreign and security policy.

Deployability

The continuing focus on reduction and transition explains NATO's most pressing problem: the lack of deployable combat forces. On paper Europe has much to offer. The member states of the European Union (EU) have approximately 1.7 million men and women under arms. Collectively, the European member states of NATO have roughly one million more. NATO members who are not EU member states, such as Turkey and—until May 2004—Poland possess respectively 630,000 and 320,000 troops. Although significant in size, they do not contribute to the overall deployability of NATO. Turkey needs its forces for internal security, i.e. the fight against the Kurdish PKK in the eastern parts of the country. Moreover, it borders high risk areas, including Iraq. Poland, like other former Warsaw Pact nations, possesses legacy forces which are not interoperable with those of NATO. Due to the dire state of their economies they lack the money to restructure forces into interoperable and professional expeditionary armed forces, capable of carrying out a wide range of missions outside their homelands. Most former Warsaw Pact states also lack the necessary defense planning capacities for force restructuring.

Most European forces are still in-place forces. This explains why only 10 to 15 per cent of NATO's forces are deployable. The 18 nations belonging to NATO's integrated military structure collectively have 238 combat brigades, including 69 U.S. brigades. Less than 80 of those are considered 'deployable,' including 29 US brigades. France could provide two or three extra brigade equivalents with approximately 10,000 troops.[1]

Relief of deployed forces is required after six months; a new deployment of a unit is considered after one year. This requires two brigades in reserve for each deployed brigade. Thus, only 13 to 15 European brigades can be deployed at once. This makes a total of approximately 40,000 troops. If France is included the number will rise to approximately 43,500. Of course, for a one-time deployment for combat missions the number could be significantly higher.

---

[1] France has regiments which are smaller than brigades, but bigger than battalions.

Small and Big Countries

How to define a small country? At first glance, the GDP of the Netherlands and Canada are roughly comparable and so are their armed forces. In addition, both countries have similar views on the use of armed force. They put emphasis on stabilization and reconstruction and have vast experience with keeping the peace. Both are reluctant to get involved in war fighting, especially with forces for land combat. Despite these similarities, Canada is considered 'big' and The Netherlands 'small.' Thus, the labels 'big' and 'small' have little relevance. Only the actual deployable *combat* capabilities at a country's disposal give some insight in its military performance and hence pertain to the label 'big' or 'small.' A country could possess one of the following types of forces:

- A *full spectrum force* comprises the full array of assets and capabilities, allowing a member state to deal with all contingencies. It allows sustained combat operations against an opponent's irregular or regular forces, and to carry out stability and reconstruction operations in an effort to keep or bring the peace in distant places. A country with a full spectrum force could provide the framework for coalition operations as well. A *framework nation* provides the backbone of an operation. Other nations "plug in."

- *Broad expeditionary capabilities* allow a country to carry out similar operations, albeit on a more modest scale. Those countries could act as a lead nation for less demanding operations. A *lead nation* is responsible for planning the campaign; it directs the strategic decision making process and provides the key elements of C4I.

- *Focused expeditionary capabilities* allow countries to contribute to a wide variety of military operations with a limited range of capabilities. Some countries may even be able to act as a lead nation for small stabilization operations in a permissive environment.

- *Selective expeditionary capabilities* allow countries to contribute with some force elements to coalition operations. The development of *niche capabilities* is the obvious choice. Niche capabilities are those scarce capabilities that complement and enhance the performance of the entire coalition and cannot usually be commonly owned.

- *Stabilization capabilities* allow countries to make a contribution to peace keeping. These countries could help funding *collective capabilities*. These collectively owned military capabilities, such as AWACS, are a prerequisite for coalition operations.

The next step is to match these types of forces with member states. As can be concluded from Table 1, the ranking depends heavily on conscription. For domestic and social reasons a number of countries are reluctant to abolish conscription (Germany and Greece). Some countries did not have conscripts by the end of the Cold War (Luxembourg, the United Kingdom). Others created professional forces during the 1990s (Belgium, The Netherlands). Most countries, however, are still in a transition phase towards strictly professional or all volunteer armed forces.

In practice those countries reluctant to abolish conscription are reluctant to deploy land forces for combat missions abroad as well; countries in a transition phase simply lack deployable land forces for combat missions. Indeed, the problem of deployability mainly applies for land forces, because these forces are traditionally filled with conscripts. Technologically advanced aircraft and vessels have always required volunteers.

Table 1: Ranking of NATO Member States: A Qualitative Assessment

Full spectrum force	USA
Broad expeditionary capabilities	UK, France after restructuring** The Netherlands
	Spain** and Italy** after restructuring
Focused expeditionary capabilities	Belgium, Canada, Denmark,** Germany,* Norway*
Selective expeditionary capabilities	Poland,* Turkey*
Stabilization capabilities	Estonia,* Bulgaria,* Czech Republic,* Greece,* Hungary,* Latvia,* Lithuania,* Luxembourg, Portugal,* Romania,* Slovenia,* Slovakia*
No capabilities	Iceland (some paramilitary and coastguard)

* = conscripts
** = transition to professional armed forces or mix of conscripts and professionals

All countries mentioned could contribute to stability operations. A country's contribution to expeditionary warfare or power projection is the real distinction. Consequentially, NATO's lack of deployable forces is worrisome, because contemporary military power is mainly used to defend one's interests abroad or to carry out stability and reconstruction operations. Thus, expeditionary capabilities for power projection are critical for contributions to international coalitions. Without those capabilities, countries could become free riders.

The U.S., the only member state with the full array of capabilities, forms a class of its own. In Europe there are important differences. Regarding defense modernization and transformation, only the British, the French and the Dutch seem well on track. Despite budget cuts and downsizing, they restructure their armed forces continuously. The United Kingdom has the most capable armed forces of all of Europe's NATO nations. In its Strategic Defense Review the UK announced various measures, such as the creation of a pool of Joint Rapid Reaction Forces drawn from the three services, to provide a rapidly deployable and militarily powerful cutting edge in crises of all kind. Other measures include new capabilities, such as larger aircraft carriers, improved strategic transport, and deployable headquarters and communications.[2]

The UK deployed almost half of its force to the Gulf region for operation *Iraqi Freedom*. Nevertheless, it turned out that British forces lacked sufficient combat support and logistics to deploy distribution and forces quickly throughout the theatre. Moreover, interoperability with American forces was a problem. The UK's *Iraq First Reflection* Report concluded that the "UK contribution was taken into the U.S. plan where it could best complement and enhance U.S. capabilities, both politically and militarily. Most of what UK forces achieved took place under the umbrella of U.S. dominance of every warfare environment."[3] There were specific shortfalls as well: "given the U.S. technological and military dominance, we should continue to track, align with and integrate U.S. developments in areas where our force balance and resources allow, particularly in terms of enhanced HQs, communications and information systems, and Combat Identification."[4]

---

[2] Ministry of Defence, *The Strategic Defence Review*, London (The Stationary Office), July 1998.

[3] Ministry of Defence (UK), *Operations in Iraq, First Reflections*, July 2003, p. 19.

[4] *Operations in Iraq*, p. 7.

Indeed, although the UK has the most capable forces in Europe, operation *Iraqi Freedom* demonstrated that British forces could not keep up with the Americans because they lacked interoperability, combat support and logistics. Nevertheless, at present only the UK is capable of leading multinational operations at division plus level.

France is a 'big' military power as well, especially after the major reconstruction of its armed forces is carried out. During the late 1990s France ran the risk of military decline to a military second tier status. In 2002 the new center-right government of President Chirac announced for $87 billion in military capital spending between 2003 and 2008. France aimed at restructuring its armed forces along similar lines as the UK. As its focus is power projection, it was decided to procure a second aircraft carrier, unmanned drones, additional combat aircraft and attack helicopters and 50 A400M transport planes, as well as new submarines and frigates.

Apart from these two major players, within Europe there are two special cases. The first is the Netherlands. As table 2 shows, the Netherlands ranks substantially higher than one would expect. The Netherlands has sea, land and air forces and a broad range of force elements, sufficient to make a meaningful contribution to a wide variety of operations. In the United Nations Mission in Ethiopia and Eritrea (UNMEE), for example, the Netherlands provided the framework for peace keeping operations. Indeed, the Dutch belong to the most important troop contributors. As a matter of fact, due to the quality and diversity of its armed forces the Netherlands is in a position to provide the benchmark for most small NATO members.

Restructuring began with the 1993 White Paper. Until then, the force posture of the Netherlands was focused on the defense of NATO territory. The White Paper concluded that although a strategic attack on NATO territory was unlikely, the world had not become a safer place. New risks had emerged. The Balkans and the Gulf regions had become permanent sources of unrest. The danger of proliferation of weapons of mass destruction and their means of delivery was real, and international terrorism and international crime were considered a growing threat. These risks, together with the scarcity of natural resources, threats to trade routes, the fact that economic prosperity depends on global stability, and the desire to relieve human suffering, would require a wide toolbox of military capabilities.

Thus, together with a decrease of the defense budget a reorientation of the task, role and mission of the armed forces took place. It was decided to leave the existing structure with naval, land and air force elements intact. Restructuring would focus on expeditionary warfare or power projection. Due to the political ambition to make a contribution to both combat operations and stability and reconstruction missions, a wide toolbox was developed. This toolbox contained a broad range of assets which would provide politicians flexibility through a wide range of options. An all-volunteer armed force was deemed necessary, because political practice prevented the use of conscripts for combat missions abroad. Moreover, it was decided to procure strategic lift and to put more emphasis on logistics and combat support. A dramatic downsizing of almost 50 per cent in terms of manpower relieved the funds necessary for the restructuring of the Dutch armed forces.

Conversely, Germany ranks lower than one would expect. Potentially, Germany is the most powerful continental power. However, it is still struggling with its legacy of the past and the integration of the former German Democratic Republic's armed forces into the Bundeswehr. One of the biggest obstacles for abolishing the draft is the impact on Germany's social system. Many young men refusing to do military service must perform duties in social service. As a consequence Germany would lose cheap labor in various sectors, with important consequences for society as a whole.

Despite the fact that Germany has set up a 60,000-strong reaction force comprising volunteer conscripts, short-service and regular personnel of the three armed services, the organization and structure of the armed forces are still mainly oriented towards traditional defense tasks.[5] Of this total there are some 50,000 army and 12,300 air force personnel. For political reasons ordinary conscripts cannot be deployed out of the country and volunteer conscripts can only be deployed in traditional low-risk peacekeeping operations. Only conscripts with an extended contract (23 instead of 12 months) can be deployed outside the country. Due to conscription and logistical shortfalls Germany, with a land force of more than 220,000, cannot deploy more than 10,000 troops for stability operations in three to four theaters of operations simultaneously.

In May 2003 new defense policy guidance was adopted, emphasizing Bundeswehr reform to execute new tasks better, stress multinational embedding, and pursue joint operations without geographical limits for the deployment of troops.[6]

Germany's struggle with force modernization reflects its political culture. Over the last half a century Germany has pursued a consistent national security policy that de-emphasizes military power as an instrument of foreign policy. Consequently, the role of the military in society has substantially decreased. After the end of the Cold War, the government could only send troops abroad for low-risk peacekeeping missions. It was only after a decision by the Constitutional Court on July 12, 1994 that the road was opened for active participation in combat missions.

Germany's struggle reflects a broader European problem, i.e. the differences in political and strategic culture between the U.S. and Europe. Europe's political system, embodied in the European Union, is a *post-modern system* with some fundamental characteristics:

- Mutual interference in each other's domestic affairs. As a result, the distinction between domestic and foreign affairs has become blurred, borders have become irrelevant and the concept of sovereignty has weakened.

- The obsolescence of armed force as an instrument for resolving disputes. Self-imposed rules of behavior have been codified and are monitored.

- Security has become based on transparency, mutual openness, interdependency and mutual vulnerability.[7]

This 'demilitarization' of relations within the system explains why most Europeans are reluctant to use armed force outside the system. Although some states in this post-modern system—notably the UK and France—behave like traditional major powers on some occasions, Germany and smaller powers have firmly embraced the norms and values embedded in this post-modern system. They emphasize the role of international institutions. They stress stabilization and reconstruction more than war fighting. The U.S, like most other countries,

---

[5] "Reaction Time," *Jane's Defence Weekly*, July 7, 1999, p. 25.

[6] *Defence Policy Guidelines*, Berlin, May 21, 2003. For an elaboration of Germany's reform efforts, see the contribution by Manfred Engelhardt in this volume.

[7] Robert Cooper, "The new liberal imperialism," *The Observer*, 7 April 2002.

is a modern state with a traditional view of sovereignty, and the role of its armed forces in protecting the nation and its interests. This contributes to misperceptions about what Europe is about and the role military power plays in European foreign and security policy.

In sum, one might label as 'big' only those countries that possess a full spectrum force or broad expeditionary capabilities. Only those countries are capable of carrying out expeditionary operations independently at various levels and could perform the duties of a lead nation. Nevertheless, distinct political and strategic cultures on both sides of the Atlantic Ocean will continue to generate different opinions about the use of military power.

The other member states are 'small.' They could make contributions to international coalitions with a focused toolbox or niche capabilities. The remaining member states have can only offer capabilities for stability operations. In some cases they might provide some logistics or (combat) support for expeditionary operations.

The new NATO members face the biggest challenges. Former Warsaw Pact countries must adapt NATO procedures and doctrine, and must invest in new assets in order to achieve a modest level of interoperability with other NATO forces. Due to the dire state of their economies, force modernization and transition to professional armed forces will be a lengthy process.

The Challenges of Modernization, Transition and Transformation

An issue much neglected is that sharp reductions could bring the force elements of individual countries below a critical mass, both in terms of commitments and economies of scale. This is a challenge for small countries. Sooner or later they have to make the choice whether they want to preserve or abandon capacities, develop a more focused toolbox or specialize on niche capabilities.

The case of the Netherlands makes this challenge for today's defense planners clear. As has been argued before, the Netherlands possesses a wide toolbox of forces to carry out combat missions, stabilization and reconstruction operations. During the 1990s, due to new missions, ongoing restructuring and an ever decreasing defense budget, the toolbox became both wider and shallower. After 2000, new budget cuts, increased operating costs due to ongoing peace keeping operations, the increased complexity of missions, enhanced readiness and sustainability requirements, and the costs of modernization and transformation presented new challenges.

Hence, the 2004 Defense Budget Statement sought a new balance between the tasks of the armed forces and the means available, in order to create affordable armed forces and the necessary funding for investments. A 5 per cent budget cut in 2003 required a reduction in the size of some force elements of 20 to 30 percent. This brought some elements under a critical mass, both in terms of commitments and economies of scale.

For example, the number of frigates will be reduced from 14 to 10. The consequences of this reduction are that a contribution to peace-keeping operations with frigates can only be carried out when units are withdrawn from standing commitments, i.e. the Standing Naval Forces of NATO or national obligations in the Antilles. Thus, in terms of commitments this force element is well below the critical mass.

Other force elements, such as the Maritime Patrol Aircraft, including those rebuilt for ground surveillance, will be abolished. A reduced number of aircraft would require the same infrastructure, logistical base and training facilities, and hence would fall below a critical mass in terms of economies of scale.

In addition, budgets cuts for 2004 have increased the problems of transformation. While force modernization will still be possible, it is not certain that the funding for transformation is sufficient. Transformation requires the government to spend 30 per cent of the budget on procurement and research and development. Unfortunately, only 20 to 25 per cent will be spent on these activities. There is not only a clear danger that the Netherlands will fall to a lower category, but that it will be deprived of armed forces meaningful as an instrument of foreign policy.

The case of the Netherlands shows that the broad toolbox approach will become unaffordable if the Government does not spend more on defense. The lesson learned is clear: due to downscaling, force elements could fall below a critical mass. In order to keep selected force elements above that critical mass and relieve funding for transformation, the choice is a focused tool box or niche capabilities. This not only requires a political decision on national ambitions but better international cooperation as well. Indeed, to be able to make a meaningful contribution the focused toolbox or niche capabilities must be brought into balance with the efforts of others.

Political Ambitions

As the case of Italy, Spain and the Netherlands each demonstrates, a country's place in the Table 1 ranking is not static. There is a clear correlation between political ambition, defense spending and the type of force required. The challenges for smaller member states are monumental. For most countries it is unlikely that defense budgets will be increased substantially. Most countries are involved in a transition to more interoperable, all volunteer professional armed forces and have to spend money on the procurement of new assets. The transition process, however, is very demanding and requires additional funding. In most cases a modest degree of modernization will be possible, while the funding for a meaningful transformation is lacking.

Governments have to make their ambitions clear to explain defense efforts to their populations and to explain future contributions to their allies. As table 2 shows, political ambitions define a nation's type of force and consequently, the required assets.

Ideally, governments must agree on political ambitions before starting a process of force restructuring. First, a government must choose a profile. A low profile focuses on stabilization and reconstruction operations only, whereas a high profile focuses on contributions to combat operations. Second, a government must determine whether it wants to become a lead nation as well. It goes without saying that only those countries with a medium to high profile are in a position to lead stability or combat operatives.

Most countries are likely to opt for a low to medium profile, with emphasis on defensive or offensive means. They may try to climb to a higher category, but due to heavy costs and bureaucratic inexperience this will be a hazardous task.

Table 2: Political Ambitions

Political ambition	Required force	Examples of required assets
Low profile, low risk (5th tier).	No capabilities for expeditionary warfare; limited capabilities for stability operations	Light infantry for stability operations, lift.
Low profile, medium risks (4th tier).	Niche capabilities for expeditionary warfare	The aforementioned assets, plus niche capabilities such as mountain troops, special operations forces, medical units, NBC protection.
Medium profile, medium risk (3rd tier).	Focused toolbox for defensive expeditionary operations and (combat) support.	The aforementioned assets, plus niche capabilities such as air defenses, ballistic missile defenses, RPV, UAV, mine hunters.
Medium profile, high risk (2nd tier).	Focused toolbox for offensive expeditionary operations.	The aforementioned assets, plus frigates, fighters, submarines, initial entry forces such as air maneuverable brigades and marines and follow-on forces such as mechanized and infantry brigades and the capability to provide the backbone of a peacekeeping operation.
High profile, high risks (1st tier).	Broad toolbox for expeditionary warfare	The aforementioned assets, plus the capability to provide the backbone of a combat operation at division plus level.
Global responsibilities	Full spectrum expeditionary capabilities	The aforementioned assets, plus strategic assets such as satellites, strategic bombers and the means to provide the backbone for coalition operations at army corps level.

Within Europe, the United Kingdom and France are likely to remain the most potent European countries. Second tier countries are Spain and Italy, but after restructuring they will enter the top league. The Netherlands is still a first tier country but may not be able to finish its job. There is a clear danger that it will fall to second or,—probably—third tier ranking. Most NATO member states, however, have a fourth of fifth tier ranking.

A country adopting a medium profile could focus on a focused toolbox or specialization. It could focus on its own niche capabilities, contribute to pools of capabilities, or transfer part of its budget to collectively owned capabilities.

In practice, for the small countries there are two basic choices. A focused toolbox requires a country to specialize in a specific type of force. A country specializing in niche capabilities will focus on complementary capabilities for expeditionary warfare and stabilization operations. Capabilities could be brought into a pool of multinational capabilities.

Developing New Capabilities

After having agreed on political ambitions and the required type of force, a government must decide which capabilities will be developed. To be able to provide a credible contribution to international coalitions, these capabilities should help correct the numerous deficiencies within NATO.

Operation *Allied Force* in 1999 underscored that Europe was unable to carry out sustained combat operations. During the Kosovo war the United States flew 65 per cent of all combat missions, provided most smart munitions, deployed most support aircraft such as tankers, launched almost all cruise missiles, was responsible for almost all strategic intelligence, and dominated the entire command and control of the air campaign. Of the European NATO members, the UK flew most combat missions, followed by France and the Netherlands, clearly reflecting the ranking mentioned above.

During the years preceding operation *Allied Force* there had been much discussion about the technology gap between the Americans and Europeans. But it was now clear that the gap was real. Operations *Enduring Freedom* and *Iraqi Freedom* confirmed this observation.

One way to define shortfalls is to identify first Essential Operational Capabilities (EOCs):

- Timely availability;
- Validated intelligence;
- Deployability and mobility;
- Effective engagement;
- Command and control;
- Logistic support;
- Survivability and force protection.

Together, these seven EOCs form a 'military capability.' To develop a focused toolbox or niche capabilities, the best approach is to identify European shortfalls within these EOCs first.[8] The shortfalls of timely

---

[8] The deficiencies mentioned are based on NATO's Defense Capabilities Initiative, the EU's Capabilities Action Program, and various supporting documents.

availability include high readiness, highly mobile and lethal forces, equipped and trained for covert and overt missions in complex terrain, such as special operations forces and mountain forces. Specialized forces such as air maneuver brigades, Special Operation Forces (SOF) and mountain troops are true niche capabilities for those smaller countries willing to run risks during expeditionary operations.

The shortfalls regarding *validated intelligence* include strategic reconnaissance (satellites); signals intelligence; early warning and distant detection; target acquisition; battlefield intelligence and strategic reconnaissance (ISTAR); and Human Intelligence (HUMINT). Small countries could develop typical niche capabilities, such as HUMINT, Unmanned Aerial Vehicles (UAV) and Remotely Piloted Vehicles (RPV).

The shortfalls of *deployability and mobility* include air and sea lift capabilities; with emphasis on wide-body aircraft and Roll on/Roll off ships; and air-to-air refueling. All of these are true niche capabilities for those countries willing to contribute to expeditionary warfare without running risks.

Effective engagement includes the following shortfalls: precision guided munitions; stand-off weaponry, including cruise missiles; and attack helicopters. Countries with fighter aircraft have no other choice but to procure precision guided munitions. Those with frigates could procure Tactical Land Attack Missiles and those with MLRS, the Army Tactical Missile System (ATMS). These niche capabilities are of interest to those countries willing to run risks during expeditionary operations.

Command and control involve the following deficiencies: secure and deployable C4 (Command, Control, Communications, Computers). As all countries with deployable forces need C4, these cannot be considered niche capabilities. Instead, they belong to the operational backbone of any country possessing a focused or broad toolbox. The same holds true for deployable division or brigade headquarters. Only deployable communication modules could be considered niche capabilities.

The shortfalls of *logistic support* involve tactical lift, notably transport helicopters; and tracking and tracing systems. The latter is a prerequisite for countries deploying forces so that tracking and tracing systems cannot be considered a niche capability. Transport helicopters and tactical transport aircraft, however, are niche capabilities. Countries willing to contribute with selective defensive means may find it attractive to invest in these capabilities.

Finally, *survivability and force protection* involves Suppression of Enemy Air Defenses; NBC protection and detection, and Combat Search and Rescue. Small countries have good opportunities to focus on one or more of these capabilities.

Europe's most pressing problem is the lack of an operational framework for large scale sustained combat operations. During the Cold War, the United States provided the backbone of the defense against the Warsaw Pact. Due to political controversies and budgetary problems the Europeans were not able to create such a backbone themselves.

Only the UK is able to provide the backbone for a division-plus size operation. Other member states, most notably France, could provide staff support to develop credible operation plans. There are, however, no European capabilities for corps-sized operations. As a first priority Europe must create command, control, communications and computers, intelligence, surveillance and reconnaissance (C4ISR) capabilities and deployable headquarters to carry out European-led operations. However, it is of utmost importance that interoperability with U.S. forces is taken into account to allow for some form of cooperation with U.S. forces. At present, however, full interoperability between U.S. and European forces is unlikely to be achieved within the next decade.

Transformation

The procurement of new capabilities, however, will not automatically result in better war fighting capabilities. Little money is spent on transformation. Only the UK and Sweden spend more than a third of their defense budgets on procurement, research and development. France spends 25 per cent; most others spend less than 20 percent. Transformation not only requires new thinking, new doctrines, and new methods of training but additional investments as well. A fundamental problem is that most member states have long-term planning cycles, focusing on the next 10 to 15 years. Transformation requires huge short-term investments, e.g. in software for new C4 systems.

Therefore, transformation demands revision of existing planning procedures. At least ten percent of the budget should be uncommitted to allow for these short-term investments.

In the U.S., force transformation is driven by concepts such as Network Centric Warfare (NCW) and its critical enabler Effects Based Operations.[9] During Operations *Enduring Freedom* and *Iraqi Freedom* the Americans applied aspects of this new method of warfare with great success. Situational awareness, provided by vastly improved computer systems for C4ISR, contributed to the synchronism, simultaneity and speed of the combined and joint operations. Land power reinforced airpower and vice versa. Everything that could be seen on the battlefield was destroyed almost instantaneously with great precision and focus. The effort was not hampered by bad weather or night time. As a result, regime changes were achieved quickly with few friendly losses and low levels of collateral damage. A similar transformation could turn NATO's armed forces into a more usable political instrument. But smaller NATO members have not fully grasped the issue of force transformation and its importance for carrying out future military operations in multinational coalitions.

In an attempt to introduce the new thinking in Europe, NATO's Prague summit approved the creation of the U.S.-proposed NATO Response Force (NRF): a rapidly deployable force, trained and equipped for this new way of warfare. The force must be fully deployable in October 2006, while the first elements should be operational in October 2004. It is a European test bed for new concepts, meant to spearhead force transformation.

For Europe the choice is between network *centric* and network *enabled* operations. Only the full spectrum force of the U.S. is capable of network centric operations, because theoretically the services can be brought into one joint operational framework and trained and equipped according to the same doctrine. As the Europeans are unlikely to close that technology gap and are likely to maintain differ-

---

[9] John Arquilla and David Ronfeldt, eds., *Networks and Netwars: the Future of Terror, Crime and Militancy*, (Santa Monica Ca.: RAND, MMR-1382, ODS, 2001); D. S. Alberts, J.J. Garska, F.P. Stein, *Network Centric Warfare: Developing and Leveraging Information Superiority*, CCRP Publication Series, 1999. E.J. Dahl, 'Network Centric Warfare and the Death of Operational Art," *Defence Studies*, Vol. 2, No. 1 (Spring 2002), pp. 1-24.

ent armed forces and doctrines, joint and combined operations must be organized in a different way. At a minimum European forces must be able to plug in to fully interoperable C4ISR. Thus network enabled operations allow for a degree of doctrinal and technological divergence. Given the state of the budgets of most European member states, network enabled operations, supported by advanced C4ISR and a modest degree of doctrinal convergence, would be a major step forward, but one that is unlikely to be achieved before 2010.

More Bang for a Euro

EU member states collectively have a gross national product roughly comparable to that of the U.S. and spend roughly 65 per cent of what Washington spends on its armed forces. The real problem is that Europeans get a disproportionately low return from their budgets in key areas such as procurement and research and development. In some areas the European allies collectively have only 10 to 15 per cent of the assets of the Americans.

If governments are not willing or able to increase defense budgets, further downsizing is a method to find the funding for force transformation. The 2003 *Defense Requirements Review* (DRR) calls for a 38 per cent reduction of land forces, a 23 percent reduction of air forces and a 21 percent reduction of maritime forces. The aim is to vastly improve the number of deployable forces. As only expeditionary capabilities matter, so called in-place land forces must be reduced substantially. More countries will be required to give up conscription and turn their armed forces into professional, all volunteer armed forces.

The next step is to develop a focused tool box or specialize on niche capabilities that can be brought into multinational pools of capabilities. In addition, member states could develop collectively owned capabilities. These are first steps towards role specialization, but this could only be successful if Europeans continue to work on defense integration. Indeed, this is the only way to overcome the challenges associated with Europe's fragmented and therefore inefficient defense spending.

As most EU member states are unlikely to increase their defense budgets substantially, the necessary money can only be found if the EU members no longer organize their defenses on a strictly national bases but strive for a common defense. As NATO is not part of Europe's integration process, a supranational approach is only possible through the EU. The 1992 Maastricht Treaty on the European Union saw the birth of the Common Foreign and Security Policy (CFSP) "which might in time lead to" a common defense. In other words, the pursuit of a common defense is an integral part of the development of the European Union. This policy objective was reconfirmed with the 1997 Amsterdam Treaty, which created the European Security and Defense Policy (ESDP).

This policy objective is especially of great importance to small countries. First, by removing defense bureaucracies in EU member states more money will be available for capabilities. But removing defense bureaucracies is only possible if Europe develops a centralized defense bureaucracy in support of supranational decision making.

Second, a European defense based on supranational decision making opens the perspective of role specialization and commonly owned capabilities. Member states could specialize on niche capabilities or a focused toolbox of a limited range of capabilities. Moreover, member states will be more willing to pool scarce resources and create more collective capabilities. Consider the following example. Country X specializes in air power, country Y in land forces and country Z in naval forces. In this case a supranational authority has the power to combine force elements of these countries into one Combined Joint Task Force. Without supranational authority, a country not willing to deploy its capabilities could effectively block the entire operation.

The developments in the field of the ESDP were quite impressive, considering the three decades it cost to establish a single European market. Two events contributed to its rapid development. First, when Yugoslavia collapsed during the early 1990s the Europeans failed to develop a common and coherent policy. Europe was not able to deal with the atrocities taking place in Bosnia following its collapse. Second, European leaders realized that Europe's inability to deal with security problems on its doorstep would have consequences that would diminish Europe's stature in the world.

This led to initiatives in 1992 by the West European Union (WEU) to reorganize European armed forces to allow force projection and the management of crises elsewhere. The WEU defined the so-called

'Petersberg tasks'—named after a meeting at the Petersberg conference site on the Rhine river near Bonn—as a first expression of the
realization that Europe should do more in the field of defense. These
tasks comprised humanitarian and rescue tasks, peacekeeping tasks and
tasks of combat forces in crisis management, including peace-making.

Of great significance was the initiative by Britain and France to give
more substance to the defense component of the ESDP. At their
meeting in December 1998 in St. Malo, French President Jacques
Chirac and British Prime Minister Tony Blair agreed that the member
states of the European Union should have a 'capacity for autonomous
European action.' The importance of the St. Malo declaration is that
it has complemented the debate on institutional matters with a discussion on capabilities, which has led to the creation of the EU Rapid
Reaction Force (EU RRF) for expeditionary operations. Following
the St. Malo summit, at the Cologne European Council in June 1999
the heads of government and state agreed that the EU must have the
ability and the capacity to take decisions for autonomous action on the
full range of Petersberg tasks, irrespective of actions taken by
NATO.[10] For that purpose they decided that the EU should have the
necessary military forces and the appropriate capabilities in the area of
intelligence, strategic transport, command and control.

EU leaders realized that the ability to decide on and conduct effectively EU-led military operations requires both a capacity for analysis
of situations and sources of intelligence, and a capability for relevant
strategic planning. Thus, during the 1999 Cologne summit the heads
of state and government considered holding regular formal and informal meetings of the defense ministers of the member states within the
EU institutional framework, and creating a Political and Security
Committee of political and military experts as well as an EU Military
Committee consisting of Military representatives that would make
recommendations to the Political and Security Committee. The
Union's leaders also realized the need for an EU military staff, including a situation center and other resources, such as a satellite center
and an Institute for Security Studies.[11]

---

[10] Cologne European Council—Presidency Conclusions, Cologne, June 3-4, 1999.

[11] Cologne European Council—Presidency Conclusions, Cologne, June 4, 1999, Press
Release: Document 150/99.

These general guidelines for developing an autonomous capacity to take decisions and to launch and conduct EU-led military operations in response to international crises were translated into more concrete decisions during the next European Council in Helsinki in December 1999. The member states decided that in order to be able to carry out the Petersberg tasks the EU must have at its disposal by the year 2003 a military force of 15 brigades or 50,000 to 60,000 persons, with the necessary command, control and intelligence capabilities as well as logistics and other combat support services. Such a military force has to be deployed rapidly within 60 days and sustainable for at least one year. This so-called Helsinki Headline Goal was supplemented by the decision to establish within the Council new political and military bodies that will enable the EU to take decisions on EU-led operations and ensure the necessary political control and strategic direction of such operations.[12] Interestingly, the number of brigades mentioned equals the total number of deployable brigades in Europe.

Under Portugal's EU Presidency in early 2000 EU defense ministers started to implement earlier decisions. An Interim Political and Security Committee as well as an Interim Military Body were established and began operating in Brussels in March 2000. The Secretary General of the Council of the EU also appointed the head of the military experts seconded by the member states to the Council Secretariat. The Military experts help the Council in its work on ESDP, and form the nucleus of the Military Committee and Military Staff, which were established under the Nice Treaty of the European Union. The implementation process continued under France's EU Presidency in the fall of 2000, and included a Force Generation Conference with the aim of establishing a rapid reaction facility. During this meeting EU defense and foreign ministers made a large leap forward in the EU's determination to develop an autonomous military capability. Although they emphasized that such a capability did not involve the establishment of a European army, they agreed to commit the necessary military capabilities to establish create a pool of more than 100,000 persons, 400 combat aircraft and 100 warships.[13]

---

[12] Helsinki European Council—Presidency Conclusions, Helsinki, December 10-11, 1999.

[13] Council-General Affairs / Defense: Military Capabilities Commitment Declaration, Brussels, October 20, 2000, Press Release No. 13427/2/00.F

Ground forces should be capable of executing the most demanding Petersberg tasks, i.e. large-scale sustained combat operations in a high-risk environment. This would include peacekeeping operations and large-scale offensive operations for defending EU interests. The Helsinki decision, however, raised many questions. First, did the figure of 50,000—60,000 include support units? A rule of thumb suggests the following composition of armed forces:

- 1/3 logistics (in the pre-deployment phase logistics could be as high as 50%);

- 1/3 combat support forces;

- 1/3 maneuver or combat forces.

The Council decision suggested that the 15 brigades included both organic logistics and combat support. Thus, only 20,000 combat forces would be available. Such a fighting force would not be sufficient to be deployed in the *most demanding* Petersberg Tasks. A rapidly deployable armed force of 50,000—60,000, which includes logistics and combat support, cannot meet the headline goal. With such a force the EU could take over the KFOR operations from NATO in the Federal Republic of Yugoslavia, but the full range of Petersberg tasks, including the most demanding would require at least 50,000—60,000 combat forces, implying a pool of 150,000—200,000 deployable troops. Depending on sustainability requirements, these numbers should be doubled or tripled. In conclusion, the present force catalogue of 100,000 indicates that sustainability is a major shortfall and that the full range of Petersberg tasks cannot be executed. Moreover, a pool of 150,000—200,000 deployable forces encompasses *all* deployable forces of EU member states.

During the EU's Nice summit in 2000 it was decided to incorporate the functions of the West European Union, with the exception of its collective defense clause, into the Treaty on the European Union. Thus, the WEU—revitalized during the 1980s to become the EU's military arm—ceased to exist as an organization for collective security, while at the same time the EU obtained a security function. During the EU's Seville summit in 2002 it was decided to include the fight against international terrorism in Europe's common foreign, security and defense policy.

A major breakthrough in the institutional development of ESDP occurred during the EU Council Meeting in Copenhagen in

December 2002, when the Council reached agreement on the so-called 'Berlin plus' arrangements and their implementation. These arrangements, described below, provide for deeper NATO-EU cooperation, address the EU's lack of specific military capabilities and planning facilities, and are a prerequisite for EU-led operations. Turkey, which considered itself excluded from the EU—NATO consultation process, had lifted the blockade of the 'Berlin Plus' arrangements in return for close cooperation with the EU on defense matters as well as an agreement concerning the role of Cyprus in ESDP.

The "Berlin plus" arrangements refer to a package of arrangements for NATO-EU cooperation. A first outline of such arrangements was developed at NATO's 1994 Brussels Summit. During this summit NATO agreed on a European Security and Defense Identity (ESDI) allowing the Europeans to use 'separable, but not separate' military capabilities for European action. Subsequently, during the 1996 Berlin ministerial meeting the North Atlantic Council took crucial steps allowing the EU to use NATO's structures for Europe-led operations. The arrangements committed NATO to provide the WEU assured access to NATO planning and command structures and access to NATO's collectively owned assets and capabilities, including 18 AWACS planes and two not yet fully operational Combined Joint Task Force Headquarters. The arrangements also identified the Deputy Supreme Allied Commander Europe (DSACEUR) to lead NATO planning and operational efforts in support of EU operations. The original arrangements did not solve all of the practical problems of transferring NATO's collective assets to the WEU, however. Consequently, some EU member states asked Washington for a 'Berlin plus' arrangement to guarantee a broader range of NATO support. The new arrangements spelled out the practicalities of 'assured access.' They also introduced a second category of 'presumed access.' In order to use the arrangements effectively, access to other, specific national assets is needed as well. For example, some member states may need access to satellite intelligence provided by others.

By 2003 all institutional arrangements were in place to carry out military operations outside the EU and NATO areas. Moreover, that year, the High Representative for the Common Foreign and Security Policy (CFSP), Javier Solana, presented a draft strategic concept, while the European Convention presented a draft constitution to be discussed during an Intergovernmental Conference launched in late 2003 under Italy's EU Presidency. Solana's strategy paper might be understood as an informal equivalent of the U.S. National Security Strategy.[14] It spells out Europe's interests, threats to those interests, and ways these should be dealt with. Significantly, the paper argues that "Pre-emptive engagement can avoid more serious problems in the future," a position welcomed by the Bush administration. Indeed, the paper underscored European understanding that power projection should be part of its CFSP.

European Capabilities

Despite institutional progress, there is little progress regarding capabilities. The 1999 NATO Washington summit launched the Defense Capabilities Initiative (DCI) to improve the quality of Europe's armed forces with a view of ensuring the effectiveness of future multinational operations "across the full spectrum of Alliance missions in the present and foreseeable future security environment with a special focus on improving interoperability."[15] The DCI identified more than 50 deficiencies. Most of these deficiencies were also mentioned in the WEU Audit of Assets and Capabilities for European Crisis Management Operations.[16]

The DCI got its European equivalent as well: the EU's Capabilities Improvement Conference of November 2001 resulted in a European Capabilities Action Plan (ECAP), which identified most of the shortfalls listed above, and pressed individual countries to make pledges to remedy them.

Unfortunately the Europeans have a bad reputation of remedying deficiencies,[17] and improvements in Europe's armed forces were not

---

[14] J. Solana, *A Secure Europe in a Better World*, European Council, Thessaloniki, June 20, 2003.

[15] NATO, *Defence Capabilities Initiative*, Press Release NAC-S(99)69, April 25, 1999.

[16] WEU Council of Ministers, Audit of Assts and Capabilities for European Crisis Management Operations: Recommendations for Strengthening European Capabilities for Crisis Management Operations, Luxembourg, November 23, 1999.

[17] During the Cold War several attempts were made to increase European defense spending and to enhance European capabilities. It seems as if history repeated itself. The so called NATO 'AD 70' study on Allied Defense in the 1970s of December 1970, listed eight priority areas covering numerous projects to enhance the capabilities against the Warsaw Pact. At the same time the European defense ministers launched a European Defense Improvement Program designed to rectify the deficiencies listed above. It soon became clear that the AD 70 list was too broad. Consequently, it was narrowed to six basic issues.

very impressive. During the 2001 spring meeting of NATO defense ministers a report was tabled indicating that the NATO allies would fully implement less than 50 percent of the force goals agreed to in the DCI. It became clear that the DCI simply was too comprehensive. Moreover, the continuously shrinking defense budgets of most European allies made clear that defense was simply not a first priority.

Consequently, during a NATO summit in 2002, the Prague Capabilities Commitment resulted in a new capacity package aimed at improving European capabilities. The DCI was narrowed down to a small number of concrete commitments. The shortfalls will be dealt with by groups of member states or consortia that will take responsibility for one or more areas:

- All deployable NATO forces with 30 days or higher readiness will be equipped with nuclear, biological and chemical defense. Poland and Hungary have the lead in correcting these deficiencies;

- A NATO air ground surveillance system must be completed by 2004. Canada, France, Italy, the Netherlands, Spain and Turkey individually committed themselves to the procurement of additional Unmanned Aerial Vehicles (UAV);

- A full set of deployable and secure C4-systems for deployable HQs will be developed;

- The number of precision guided munitions will be increased by 30 per cent by 2005. The Netherlands forms a consortium together with Canada, Denmark, Belgium and Norway to achieve this goal;

- Suppression of Enemy Air Defenses (SEAD) will be increased by 50 per cent by 2005. Spain and The Netherlands are responsible for further action;

- Strategic air lift will be increased by 50 per cent by 2004. Germany will lease C17 air lifters and leads a consortium that will create a pool of air transport capabilities;

- Air-to-air refueling will be increased by 50 per cent by 2005. Denmark and Norway take the lead;

- Deployable logistics and combat service support will be increased by 25 per cent by 2005. These are national responsibilities.

The ECAP follows a similar approach. Consortia of member states try to remedy deficiencies. There is considerable overlap, but there are additional projects as well. Portugal will lead a consortium to increase the number of Special Operations Forces; Germany is leading an effort to improve Combat Search and Rescue; France leads efforts to create new space assets; and both medical units and tactical ballistic missile defense will be dealt with by consortia led by the Netherlands.

Both the PCC and the ECAP provide the small member states a broader concept for developing a focused toolbox and niche capabilities. However, to be successful, the initiatives of NATO and the EU should be mutually reinforcing and consequently harmonized. If this is done in a pragmatic way, correcting the shortfalls is possible. This is the task of the EU-NATO Working Capability Group. This group has the so-called Capability Development Mechanism at its disposal to oversee the development of capabilities and to coordinate the efforts of NATO and the EU.

The development of selected capabilities will cost approximately €42 billion for the improvements mentioned below.[18] This spans a ten-year period, requiring an investment of €4.2 billion per year implying a 10 per cent increase of the procurement budget.

Shortfall	Number of systems	Procurement costs in billion €
Strategic transport	225	19
Air-to-air refueling	20-30	5-7.5
Suppression of enemy air defenses	20-40	2-4
Electronic warfare	8-12	1.6-2.4
Air ground surveillance	4-8	1.4-2.8
All weather strategic theater surveillance capabilities	12 x 4 (Predators)	0.3
	13 x 4 (Global Hawk)	0.45-0.75
Combat search and rescue	12-24 (helicopters)	0.6-1.2
Electronic intelligence/ signals intelligence	4-8	2-4
TOTAL		**32–42**

Divergent Views

Despite this activity, the number of Europe-led operations is not impressive. During the early 1990s the WEU carried out a naval operation to enforce the UN embargo against Iraq. In 1992, the WEU

---

[18] Calculations by Frans Osinga of the Clingendael Centre for Strategic Studies.

became involved in the enforcement of the UN embargo of the former Yugoslavia, first in the Adriatic Sea, then along the river Danube. In 1994 the WEU was requested to organize a police force in the EU-administered city of Mostar. During the late 1990s the Union asked WEU-support in planning the Multinational Advisory Police Element (MAPE) in Albania, organizing a de-mining operation in Croatia, and monitoring the situation in Kosovo through imagery provided by the WEU Satellite Center.

A chance to carry out more demanding operations came in 1997. Albania was on the brink of civil war due to the collapse of its pyramid investment schemes. The WEU's reluctance to organize a force indicated that the organization had no real role to play in the new Europe. There was evidently no political will to carry out a large-scale European-led military operation in what was considered a high-risk environment.

In March 1997 the Security Council authorized Italy to lead a 7,000-strong multinational peace force in Albania. This clearly undermined the development of the CFSP, as the 'S' of security within the CFSP remained in fact a dead letter. Not surprisingly, the Union was criticized by the Americans for being unable to deal with security risks in its own backyard.

Immediately after the activation of the 'Berlin plus' arrangements, the Union could start the planning to take over the peace keeping operation in the former Yugoslav Republic of Macedonia and indicated its willingness to lead a military operation in Bosnia, following SFOR. This marked the end of NATO operation *Allied Harmony* in the former Yugoslav Republic of Macedonia and the subsequent handover of the mission to the EU. On March 31, 2003 the EU formally launched operation *Concordia*, with 320 peacekeepers. The operation made use of NATO assets and capabilities. This operation was followed by a 200 strong police mission in October, codenamed *'Proxima.'* In addition, the EU undertook its first military operation on June 5 2003. With 1100 military personnel the objective of operation *'Artemis'* was to create a stable situation in the eastern Congolese province of Bunia and to put a halt to the human rights violations that were taking place.

The difficulties of organizing European-led operations are an expression of considerable political problems concerning the implementation of ESDP. The debate over the definition of the Petersberg tasks explains Europe's problem. On the one hand there is the minimalist position. EU members with a strong transatlantic leaning such as the Netherlands, traditionally favor a limited interpretation of the Petersberg tasks. In order to ensure U.S. participation in more demanding crises, they wish to carry out only small-scale operations at the lower end of the conflict spectrum. They put much emphasis on avoiding unnecessary duplication with NATO, i.e. they do not want to set up separate military capabilities and structures. Governments reluctant to get involved in combat missions, such as Germany, favor a limited interpretation of the Petersberg tasks as well.

On the other hand there is the maximalist position. Members with a strong European orientation, such as France, favor military capabilities to carry out these tasks throughout the entire conflict spectrum. They point out that even small-scale operations could take place at the high end of the conflict spectrum. These countries argue that Europe needs capabilities to fight and prevail in large scale combat operations in distant places.

Due to the Iraqi war new divisions in Europe have emerged. Spain, Italy and most central and east Europeans supported the United States and the United Kingdom, while a German-French alliance opposed the policies of President Bush and Prime Minister Blair. As a direct consequence new initiatives were taken for close European defense cooperation. On April 29, 2003 the heads of state and government of France, Germany, Belgium and Luxembourg gathered for a summit in Brussels in an attempt to form a European Security and Defense Union.[19] It was argued that American unilateralism demonstrated that the European Union has no other choice but to develop a credible foreign, security and defense policy. The EU must be able to speak with one voice and fully play its role in the international scene. This would require a credible security and defense policy. The transatlantic relationship would remain a strategic priority, but a genuine partnership between the EU and NATO was considered a prerequisite for a more equal partnership between Europe and America.

Nevertheless, during the months following Operation *Iraqi Freedom*, European leaders began to realize that these divisions would

---

[19] Declaration of the Heads of State and Government of Germany, France, Luxembourg and Belgium on European Defence, Brussels, April 29, 2003.

not only marginalize Europe, but could also jeopardize Europe's integration process, with severe economic implications. This resulted in a new effort of reconciliation between the leaders of France, Germany in the United Kingdom during a summit in Berlin on September 20, 2003, and a few days later between German Chancellor Schroeder and President Bush in New York. Thus, a slow consensus is emerging about the need of European unity and equal partnership with the U.S., based on more capable European defenses.

The Need to Overcome Differences

Only through enhanced defense cooperation within the EU can NATO be strengthened. This requires the major European powers and the U.S. to set aside their differences over European defense. The litmus test for Europe's transformation process is the further development of the NATO Response Force (NRF) and the question how it interacts with the EU's Rapid Reaction Force. Unfortunately, the development of a response force has potentially devastating consequences for the further development of European capabilities, and consequently transatlantic relations. Defense Secretary Donald Rumsfeld's original proposal, discussed at the informal NATO meeting of defense ministers in Warsaw in September 2002, mentioned a force for the most challenging missions, consisting of an air component capable of carrying out 200 combat air sorties a day, a brigade-sized land force component, and a maritime component up to the size of NATO's standing naval forces. The force would consist of up to 21,000 total personnel. It would be capable of fighting together on 7-30 days notice anywhere around the world. The NRF would draw its forces from the pool of European high readiness forces. Although troop rotation was mentioned in Rumsfeld's white paper, it later turned out that the plan envisioned three response forces. The three forces would rotate and would have different levels of readiness. Only the stand-by forces would be deployable. Consequently, a total of 63,000 troops would be required; exactly the number of forces required to fulfill the Headline Goal.

As the response force draws from the same, limited pool of deployable forces, the NRF could undermine Europe's effort to develop a capability for autonomous action. Much remains unclear about the exact relationship between the two forces. However, some American officials insist on NATO's 'right of first refusal,' so that the Alliance could effectively block the use of units both assigned to the response force and to the EU's reaction forces. They also favor 'transfer of authority' of the stand-by force to a NATO joint-force commander at an early stage. This would deprive the Europeans from using their most capable forces for independent action. Finally, some officials favor a division of labor whereby the NRF is geared for high-intense combat and expeditionary strike missions, and the European force focuses on peacekeeping tasks. As both forces draw from the same pool of forces, this option, which deprives Europe of the capability to carry out operations in the upper spectrum, is a non-starter.

As European capabilities are limited, the NATO Response Force could thus effectively undermine the EU Rapid Reaction Force and hence attempts to develop credible European foreign, security and defense policies. An important task for NATO's new Supreme Allied Commander Transformation is to reconcile both efforts. The EU-NATO Capabilities Working Group should play a key role in harmonizing the PCC and the ECAP. For that purpose the Capability Development Mechanism should be fully developed.

If this process is mismanaged, the whole effort to forge more capable European defenses will once again be stalled. This will not only undermine the prospects of Europe as a strategic partner, but will also deprive Europe from important instruments to transform its armed forces into a useable instrument of its foreign and security policy and to create more operability with U.S. forces. Indeed, because transformed forces hold the promise that wars can be waged quickly and decisively with less risk for friendly forces and collateral damage, it is clear that they fit Europe's political culture better than do its existing forces.

Conclusion

Small countries have limited budgets and small defense bureaucracies. Their capacity to restructure is limited. They will find it hard to restructure their forces across the board. Those countries that wish to restructure their armed forces have no other choice but to take draconian measures. To spend enough money on restructuring they must—depending on their political ambitions—develop a focused toolbox, focus on niche capabilities or contribute to collectively owned capabilities and assets for power projection or expeditionary warfare. One of Europe's problems is inefficient defense spending. One way of dealing with this is defense integration, which will only be possible though the European Union. This requires the big member states to strive for transatlantic partnership though the development of NATO and the EU as complementary and mutually reinforcing institutions.

Chapter 7

Transatlantic Industrial Cooperation as a Tool for Transformation: A Case of Compelling Logic, But Limited Short-Term Prospects

Jeffrey P. Bialos and Stuart L. Koehl

During the 1990s, a new policy paradigm emerged that viewed enhanced transatlantic defense industrial cooperation—increased supplier globalization among a circle of close friends—as a useful tool for promoting coalition warfare, force transformation (then called the revolution in military affairs), and competition in consolidated defense markets. This conceptual approach was articulated and gained currency on both sides of the Atlantic as an alternative to a "fortress like " approach to defense industries, with little cooperation and autarky as the prevailing model.

In fact, during the Clinton Administration, efforts were made to translate this new vision into practice. There was initial progress—several years of effort in the late 1990s—in what would undoubtedly be a long-term process of shifting away from the prevailing, protectionist approach to defense industries, and overcoming enormous institutional and culture forces against change. Specifically:

- Measures were adopted to address existing impediments to globalization, and to put in place the regulatory "hard wiring" to facilitate defense industrial globalization. These included the adoption of bilateral Declarations of Principles (U.S.-United Kingdom and U.S.-Australia) and initial reforms of U.S. defense trade controls.

- On the supply side of the equation, a number of ground-breaking transactions were structured and approved—notably BAE's acquisitions in the United States and a joint venture between Raytheon and Thales.

- On the demand side, major international cooperative programs were conceived and executed, including the FA-35 Joint Strike Fighter ("JSF"), Medium Extended Air Defense System ("MEADS"), a theatre missile defense system, and Multifunctional Information Distribution System ("MIDs"), the next generation Link 16 system for secure communications and data.

However, several years into the 21st century, little additional real progress has been made in further implementing this agenda. In fact, given the significant changes in the security environment (September 11 and Operation *Iraqi Freedom*) and the change of Administrations in Washington, the shift toward this new paradigm has languished, and in some areas, past progress has been reversed—buried under other priorities from missile defense to Iraq to terrorism. Indeed, given broader geopolitical developments, including the continuing transatlantic rift over Iraq, there are a series of centrifugal forces threatening to decouple the United States and its European allies.

In the context of this very different environment, this essay explores the prospects of the cooperative paradigm described above becoming reality. As discussed herein, transatlantic supplier integration will probably occur over the long term; at some point, three or four multi-country prime contractors are likely to emerge, competing in a broader transatlantic market. This model continues to make economic sense, and potentially could produce salutary policy benefits, including greater support for coalition warfare. Indeed, without it, divergences in military transformation and industrial capabilities across the Atlantic—driven in large part by the expanding gap in defense budget outlays between Europe and the United States?—threaten to exacerbate the existing capabilities gap and undermine efforts to coalition warfare altogether (see Figure 1, below). Simply put, stagnant or declining European defense budgets, and especially European under-investment in defense research and development, likely will perpetuate and exacerbate the capabilities gap—especially in critical transformational areas like command, control, communications, computers and intelligence ("C4I").

Figure 1   U.S. and NATO Defense Spending, 2002-2006 (est.)

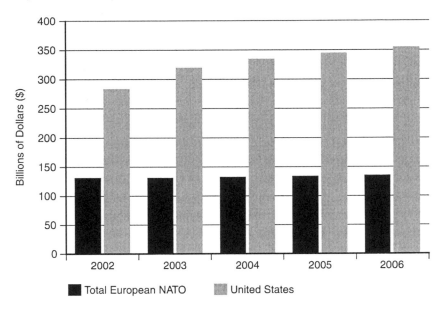

Nevertheless, as discussed below, there is little likelihood of this vision becoming reality in the near-to-medium term. Neither the U.S. nor Europe is ready today—in political, institutional and regulatory terms—for major globalization transactions; the hard wiring is not in place, the support of U.S. and European leaders is limited at best, and they have—through acts of omission and commission—stymied any progress toward supplier globalization in the last three years (See Figure 2, below).

The reality is that in defense markets—the most protected in the world— the scope and speed of supplier globalization is very much a function of the attitudes and policies of governments. Governments are, after all, the customers, the financiers and the regulators of defense industries. Moreover, the obstacles to defense industrial cooperation are daunting ones, and require a significant allocation of leadership resources to be overcome.

Today in the United States, there appears to be little or no active support for supplier globalization within the Administration. There are few, if any, statements of support, and few actions in this arena. Hence, the leadership necessary to overcome bureaucratic, cultural and political barriers does not exist, and the old paradigm—essentially a pattern of conduct one can characterize as defense autarky—continues to be in place. There are powerful institutional forces in favor of domestic sourcing and limited technology sharing from Department of Defense bureaucracies and Congress that dominate in times like these—when there is little support for shifting toward a new paradigm.

In Europe, whatever support exists for transatlantic industrial cooperation is being sorely tested by the perception of U.S. unilateralism on a host of issues and in a host of forums. European countries are gradually shedding their own nationalistic tendencies in this arena and moving toward an integrated European approach to defense—slowly, ploddingly, but inevitably—from armaments cooperation to industry, up to and including the now likely establishment of an European Union armaments agency. This evolution of a European defense identity can happen in a way that supports and strengthens NATO, coalition war fighting and open markets or moves instead toward European defense autarky and little cooperation ands views European defense cooperation as a means to create a "counterbalance" to the United States. Today, it unfortunately appears that U.S. actions—across a broad array of issues—are not only encouraging European defense integration, but are also encouraging Europe to go its own way in armament development and industrial policy. In other words, U.S. actions and policies are fueling impulses toward a Eurocentric approach to defense.

Thus, while strategic and economic logic suggests that transatlantic industrial cooperation in defense makes sense and is likely in the long term to be a useful tool for facilitating defense transformation and coalition warfare, forward movement is not likely again unless there is real leadership on this issue that highly values about having strong transatlantic allies and meaningful coalition war fighting capabilities.

The Rationale for Transatlantic Industrial Cooperation

A. Why do we or should we care about defense industrial cooperation?

- Industrial cooperation sustains the transatlantic relationship in tough times (geopolitical benefits) and enhances coalition war fighting capability (military benefits).

- It helps North Americans and Europeans meet the difficult challenge of promoting competition in consolidated defense markets, by stimulating affordability and innovation. The empirical evidence is clear that competition in defense markets —as in all markets— drives down prices, helps keep programs on schedules and creates incentives for innovation.

- Industrial cooperation makes good sense in era when the U.S. cannot support as many suppliers as would be desirable; even in an ongoing wartime buildup, the budgets cannot sustain the present industrial base—and further rationalization is necessary.

- Defense transformation requires technological innovation in armaments, and yet the continuing industrial consolidation makes it difficult to sustain the competition that can fuel such innovation. Only robust and competitive suppliers can meet the need for these types of transformational requirements

The U.S. also wants to avoid the emergence of a Fortress Europe/Fortress America in defense that will further erode the transatlantic security relationship. Open markets and integrated suppliers that compete in these markets help to promote broader geopolitical integration.

Europe also should favor this type of cooperation for similar reasons, plus the following additional ones:

- Europe on its own will likely continue to produce (as it has historically) second best military solutions for its war fighter (at higher prices) and face a perpetual capabilities gap relative to the United States.

- Without U.S. technology sharing, the gap between U.S. and European military capabilities is likely to increase in the future due to the accelerating pace and degree of U.S. transformational spending on R & D and the chronic under-investment and lack of coordination in European defense R & D.

Back to First Principles: Supplier Cooperation and The Bigger Picture

As good a case as there is for this new industrial cooperation paradigm, it is only a means to an end. In other words, defense industrial cooperation only is important in terms of policy if:

- One highly values the transatlantic relationship and believes in the importance of coalition warfare;

- One cares about maintaining open defense markets to promote competition rather than having domestic autarky;

- One really cares about the economics of defense budgets and appreciate that budget constraints necessitate this approach: and

- One is willing to engage in the type of technology sharing to make industrial cooperation a reality.

Hence, any discussion of supplier integration and cooperation must necessarily turn to first principles. Here, the reality is that the Bush Administration's overall approach and specific policies have, at best, been lukewarm or mixed with respect to the importance of the trans-Atlantic security relationship and coalition war fighting. At the very least, in the post-September 11 era of other priorities, these goals have been submerged.

Indeed, September 11 and Iraq have essentially sucked the oxygen out of defense policy—there is little room now for focus on other priorities. Even transformation of our military forces—now gaining traction again—has taken a back seat to ongoing operational requirements.

At the highest level, many have perceived a continued sense of unilateralism by the Administration. While the Administration does voice support for multilateral approaches in security, some of its voices suggest real limits to this support.[1]

---

[1] See, e.g., Remarks of Vice President Richard Cheney to Heritage Foundation (October 10, 2003) (www.whitehouse.gov/news/releases/2003/10/20031010-1.html). In the speech, Vice President Cheney appeared to equate multilateral approaches with a requirement of "unanimous international consent" and suggested that acting in concert with others can lead to "[w]eakness and drift and vacillation in the face of danger" that invites attacks. In contrast, he suggested that acting alone can produce "strength and resolve and decisive action" that can defeat attacks before they can arrive on our soil.

Certainly, it does not seem productive to have a primarily unilateral policy and disdain global institutions in a multilateral world. In the short-and-long term, this approach will have significant costs and risks for U.S. national interests. While it is always hard to put a price tag on these items, today at least it can be stated authoritatively that U.S. actions—largely alone—in Iraq have imposed the complete burden of $87 billion on the United States—with no opportunity for burden sharing. If reaction to this supplementary spending bill is any indication, the public appetite for additional defense spending increases in the context of a "go-it-mostly-alone" approach may not be unlimited.

The Administration's commitment to coalition warfare is also at best limited. While the Administration talks about "coalitions" of the willing building real coalitions for warfare and fighting together can not be done on an ad hoc basis and also will require diplomacy and skill. It really is a test of leadership to forge these types of real and enduring coalitions.

In fact, in a purely military sense, the U.S. does not need allies. The U.S. has and will continue to have qualitatively and quantitatively superior forces for the indefinite future. But, as the recent war shows, U.S. force is not unlimited, and thus it does need allies and coalitions—and not just those of the willing. Yet, today, the United States still cannot fight wars in which its allies have a truly significant role; U.S. forces are simply not interoperable with those of its allies. And the more robust U.S. spending and transformational efforts will probably increase the interoperability gap in the near to mid term.

Transatlantic Defense Cooperation: Realities & Obstacles

Given these first principles, it is not surprising that transatlantic cooperation and supplier globalization have had a relatively low priority. Specifically:

- There have been virtually no statements on supplier globalization—no public pronouncements encouraging supplier linkages or signaling a hospitable environment for them.

**Figure 2   European Acquisitions of U.S. Defense Assets:
Deals Over $100 Million**

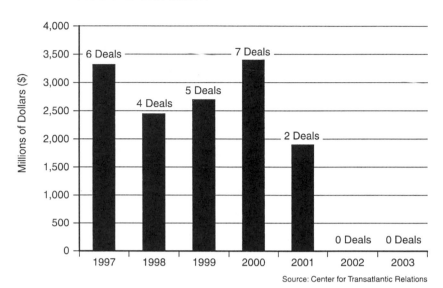

Source: Center for Transatlantic Relations

- There have been no significant transatlantic acquisitions or mergers in defense since the change of administrations. Indeed, in the last two years (2002-2003), there has not been a single foreign acquisition of a U.S. defense asset of $100 million or above; only a few BAE North American acquisitions at lower levels have occurred. (See Figure 2 above.)

- The critical impediment is technology sharing. If anything, the "releasability" of U.S. technologies to allied nations—what are we willing to share—became more difficult after September 11.

- There has been little focus on international armaments cooperation. The reality today is little ongoing cooperation with allies in armaments development and production—and continued autarky in the U.S. and growing autarky in Europe. Administration statements on international cooperation primarily focus on the JSF program– which today constitutes most of the cooperation the United States has ongoing (in dollar terms) with its allies. While the Administration has proposed missile defense cooperation, it has not to date been forthcoming.

There are some positive developments. The Bush Administration has continued to seek Declarations of Principles with other nations (Sweden and Italy, to name a few) and to expand this process. It also has quietly entered into understandings in some areas such as defense priority allocation (agreeing to reciprocal measures to facilitate giving priority treatment to allied contracting needs). Moreover, the Bush Administration used considerable "leadership" resources to fight off proposals for even more protectionist legislation concerning defense programs (which would, if enacted, have further reduced the use of foreign talents and components for the benefit of the U.S. war fighter).

Further, on the "demand" side of the market, there have been efforts to start additional cooperative programs or allow foreign participation in existing programs that would deepen transatlantic engagement. This includes missile defense (where, as discussed below, technology transfer issues have arisen), the Navy's broad area maritime surveillance/ unmanned aerial vehicle effort (i.e., an integrated solution for capability to replace for the existing maritime P-3 flight) and a possible Littoral Combat Ship program drawing on capabilities especially in northern Europe.

But overall, the agenda has not moved markedly forward. Moreover, steps like the Bush Administration's decision to exclude firms from non-coalition partner countries from the Iraqi reconstruction programs are not helpful in promoting defense industrial cooperation.

European developments reinforce these realities. In Europe today, governments are focused inward—on developing a European defense identify in terms of policy, R & D spending, and armaments development. This focus certainly has a greater priority than transatlantic cooperation in many European quarters.

In short, the bottom line is painfully clear: without leadership in support of supplier globalization and cooperation, neither the United States nor Europe is likely to make progress in light of the range of difficult problems. Bottom-up industrial combinations alone are not sufficient; top-down governmental actions are required. Given present priorities, this seems unlikely in either the United States or Europe.

A. The Technology Transfer Conundrum

Given the U.S. lead in many areas in spending and development, the reality is that U.S. technology sharing is vital to ensure Europe acquires enhanced capabilities and also can improve its interoperability. This is particularly the case in C4ISR and other transformational areas (precision munitions) where the U.S. lead is probably growing.

Regrettably, however, the U.S. willingness to share technology—across Administrations—has been very limited, in large part due to a system of export controls and related processes that inhibit sharing in various ways. This is a bipartisan problem: efforts at reform have spanned several Administrations and have been met by a largely reluctant bureaucracy. The problem has been evident for many years. The Clinton Administration announced the Defense Trade Security Initiative (DTSI), a package of licensing reforms that included country-specific ITAR waivers, a series of broad "global" licenses and other measures. The Bush Administration has built on these efforts, and is now in the process of its own National Security Council-led review (NSPD-19) of these issues—especially as they relate to transatlantic cooperation and the need for enhanced coalition war fighting capabilities. Despite the efforts of several Presidential Administrations, however, there continue to be serious and worsening problems. One has a sense of "déjà vu" all over again when approaching these "tired" issues.

While the problems in this area are manifold and complex—and truly bipartisan in nature—the key issues are as follow:

- U.S. armaments cooperation policy continues to be divorced from technology transfer policy. The U.S. commits at senior levels of government to cooperative efforts like the JSF and Missile Defense only to have them undermined by the administration of our export control and related systems. Today, U.S. credibility in the area of cooperative armaments is extremely low and our most significant efforts in this arena are struggling and at risk. Although international participation is critical to JSF, the program is foundering on the shoals of overly restrictive technology sharing with key allied governments, including even the United Kingdom. Missile defense, a key Administration priority, provides the most dramatic case in point. Notwithstanding the U.S. commitment to this capability and to ensuring international participation in it, the technology transfer issues have emerged as a critical impediment and little progress has been made in over a year in facilitating cooperation. More recently, the U.S. endorsed the concept of a NATO Response Force but appears not to have considered the technology transfer implications of a transformational, multinational force intended to be seamlessly interoperable with U.S. forces.

- There is also a dichotomy between what senior leadership says it will do and wants to do, and what is done in practice in the bureaucracy. The real problem is developing an approach and applying it throughout a bureaucracy that continues to operate under an old paradigm

The Clinton Administration tried to address the licensing issues through the Defense Trade Security initiative (DTSI), including:

- ITAR exemptions for close allies pursuant to DOPS

- Global licensing agreements designed to facilitate significant transatlantic projects, programs and joint industrial activities, joint ventures and the like.

- Process reforms to speed up procedures and create some process transparency.

Unfortunately, these reforms have to date not been implemented fully and have in some ways been counterproductive.

- The idea of country-specific exemptions for close allies, while promising, has been slowed by congressional opposition. While the Bush Administration has in fact pursued this agenda and signed such exemptions with the UK and Australia, a minority in Congress are threatening to derail it by refusing to grant relief from legislation that creates unrealistic standards for such exemptions.

- Similarly, while the idea of large, blanket licenses for major programs has promise, it too has been ineffective. The only such major license issued to date, on the JSF program, was riddled with provisos that undermined the very purpose of this type of license and imposed significant and new compliance burdens. There are real questions about this model for the future. Some believe it is likely never to be used again.

- Moreover, some successful U.S. efforts—such as reducing approval times—may have actually been counterproductive. First, this initiative has resulted in a greater number of restrictive provisos. Second, companies are now taking much longer to prepare licenses in anticipation of trying to get them through and offering the needed detail required.

- Moreover, since September 11, technology release appears to have become more restrictive—especially in areas like electro optics—and there is greater scrutiny of individual cases.

- While the Bush Administration has some "change" initiatives underway, including NSDP-19, and is introducing some needed structural and management reforms into the traditional defense trade control bureaucracies (State Department Directorate of Trade Controls and the Pentagon's Defense Trade Security Administration), different bureaucratic mechanisms have proven to be significant hurdles to technology transfer to close allies. The Low Observable/ Counter Low Observable ("LO/CLO") review group at the Department of Defense has become a significant roadblock in a broad range of technology areas. Its ambit is very broad in scope (not just LO/CLO technologies but any related capability), it has no deadlines, and its standards appear based on industrial rather than the national security considerations set forth in the Arms Export Control Act. Similarly, decision-making on anti-tamper controls (e.g., which would prevent backward engineering of a product) threatens to undermine cooperation. These decisions are made by different Pentagon bureaucracies outside of the ambit of the Defense Department's Defense Technology Security orbit and through different standards.

Underlying all of this is a sense that defense industrial protectionism is still a fundamental hallmark of U.S. policy. While the U.S. Arms Export Control Act states that sales should be denied on national security grounds (i.e., that such sales materially contribute to the capabilities of U.S. adversaries), the bureaucracy often seems to operate on an industry policy basis (i.e., protecting and maintaining U.S. technology even *vis-à-vis* close allies). These problems are apparent in the NATO Advanced Ground Surveillance (AGS) program, where the questions of cooperative radar development—on the SOSTAR/MP/RTIP capability needed to track ground moving vehicles—have been plagued by a dispute over T/R modules involving the LO/CLO review committee. A number of the Prague Capability Commitments and other needed NATO capabilities, from precision munitions to missile defense, are likely to be threatened by these types of decisions. Similarly, C4ISR is likely to be a fertile battleground for technology transfer problems.

The hard question is what to do to improve technology sharing prospects. Plainly, there are no quick or easy fixes here. We cannot solve this problem through a rule change or review of the Munitions List. Several observations need to be made here:

First, both the Clinton and Bush Administrations have been following a path of incremental reform rather than a new model. The new model path is very hard to implement, taking many years and addressing congressional issues. The incremental path is easier, but the question now is whether it works. The evidence to date is not promising.

In that case, should the U.S. really be looking at a "Cabrini Green" approach to ITAR reform? (Cabrini Green was a low-income housing project in Chicago rampant with crime, drugs and many problems. After years of various incremental approaches, the residents themselves petitioned the government to "blow it up" and start from scratch. This was done, and the major problems were addressed through a holistic alternative approach, offering other forms of housing to its residents).

Finally, ITAR waivers are not terribly popular and are hard to negotiate. But suppose one could take decisions out of the hands of bureaucrats concerning exports of technology to allies with strong export control systems and enforcement mechanisms, and who are not perceived as security risks. The U.S. could then move to a new model of "trust countries" and trusted companies in those countries. In effect, to adopt an accounting type model—whereby the United States audits the companies for compliance on re-exports and security, but eliminates case by case review. Perhaps the U.S. ought to rebuild around this concept.

B. The Demand Side of the Ledger: Tendencies toward Autarky

Industrial cooperation cannot stand by itself. Integrated supplier chains do not make sense unless there is real transatlantic demand—either a greater number of cooperative programs or more open markets. Today, there are serious impediments to these types of developments.

On the U.S. side, there continues to be little significant European participation at the prime level in U.S. programs and limited European participation in the first sub-tier. There is continued reluctance to rely on foreign systems/capabilities; the old protectionist paradigm still operates. Significantly, U.S. transformational programs have little or no foreign participation, thus increasing both the capabilities and interoperability gaps over time.

Moreover, the European market for developed U.S. solutions is becoming more challenging. The combination of circumstances—the consolidation toward two large primes—creates an impetus toward "fortress" like conduct in Europe, with politically and industrially motivated buying. There have always been significant national preferences in Europe, with "national" buying. This is gradually being replaced with "European better value" buying. The prospect of a "Europe first" procurement reform program, creating a larger European market, figures to advance better value buying but is also likely to create incentives for European buying. Moreover, U.S. sales to large western European countries and to "old" NATO countries have been trending downward over the last decade, and most U.S. sales today to Eastern Europe include significant surplus equipment.

In short, the environment on both sides of the Atlantic suggests that it is easy to sell developed solutions—especially at the systems or top subsystem level—into foreign markets, nor will it be in the future.

Needless to say, this difficult market context has strategic implications for defense firms on both sides of the Atlantic. One could conclude that it is too hard and not worth the effort to try to market products overseas. Some have undoubtedly concluded that. Others do not share that view, but rather believe that firms can operate within this mixed market and geopolitical context to create "winning" or "yes-able" propositions from a business, regulatory, and security standpoint in carefully selected business areas. The challenge is determining the types of approaches that can be structured to facilitate access to these markets in challenging times. Increasingly, the tendency is to go "local"—and create a local presence with technology, market presence and strong customer relationships—rather than market "developed solutions" from overseas. In other words, it probably is easier to "buy" into these markets—through equity acquisitions or collaborations with large, established local firms—than directly sell in the near future.

Conclusions

Industrial cooperation can be a potentially useful policy tool for solidifying the transatlantic relationship, facilitating coalition war fighting capabilities and military transformation, and improving competitiveness and cost effectiveness in defense acquisition. However, this policy tool is not a panacea. It is only effective when both sides of the Atlantic really care about the underlying security and economic goals discussed herein, and are willing to apply scarce leadership resources to address the difficult underlying impediments and shift the paradigm from industrial autarky toward technology sharing.

Frankly speaking, the notion of broad, significant change in this area—to advance seriously the paradigm of defense industrial cooperation—is a hard sell in the current environment. In the short term, the appropriate focus might perhaps be on particular programs and cooperative forms of engagement, and utilizing these efforts as "organizing" approaches to prioritize and facilitate defense industrial cooperation. The NATO Response Force now being established, for example, offers opportunities for "win-win" scenarios. This small, spearhead expeditionary force –designed to promote capability enhancement and transformation—can perhaps be an impetus for a select number of armaments and other initiatives to enhance coalition war fighting capability. These initiatives can in turn be a focal point for defense industry cooperation that supports coalition war fighting goals. A few successes here could potentially serve to showcase the merits of supplier globalization as a policy tool, and foster its expansion in the future. The challenge for the Administration is to apply the needed resources, especially in terms of leadership focus (with an admittedly crowded agenda) to "jump start" this type of effort.

Chapter 8

The Defense Industry and Transformation: A European Perspective

Andrew D. James

In NATO and in the European Union, the shortfall between European capabilities and European political and military aspirations is a source of growing concern. In November 2002, the NATO Prague Summit adopted a Capabilities Commitment to ensure that NATO will in the future have the military capabilities required for the full range of its missions. The new NATO Response Force is to act as a catalyst for change and an essential element of NATO's transformation agenda, focusing on and promoting improvements in NATO capabilities, The creation of the new NATO post of Supreme Allied Commander for Transformation will give further impetus to the process. In parallel, the European Union's Helsinki Headline Goal and the European Capability Action Plan (ECAP) process has sought to secure the necessary capabilities to fulfill the Petersberg tasks within the European Security and Defense Policy (ESDP).

There is a widespread recognition of the need to broaden and deepen armaments cooperation, both within Europe and across the Atlantic, if European governments are to meet these capabilities shortfalls.[1] This chapter argues that Europe will only meet its capabilities shortfalls through a combination of strong European efforts complemented by transatlantic armaments cooperation. Europe needs to build "Towers of Excellence" in those capability areas that are critical to its NATO commitments and the implementation of the ESDP. A strengthened European technological and industrial base is also the best way to ensure that future transatlantic armaments cooperation is balanced and in European interests. There should be no doubt that

---

[1] See, for instance: "Defence and security in an uncertain world," Keynote speech by NATO Secretary General Lord Robertson to Forum Europe, Brussels, May 17, 2002 and *The Future of the Transatlantic Defense Community, Final Report of the CSIS Commission on Transatlantic Security and Industrial Cooperation in the Twenty-First Century*, Center for Strategic and International Studies, 2003 (Washington, DC).

European governments will need to acquire U.S. technologies selectively. Simply put, European defense R&D and procurement budgets will make it impossible to keep pace with U.S. technological developments across the full range of capabilities. The pressures for closer armaments cooperation (both within Europe and across the Atlantic) are considerable. Europe's relatively limited spending on defense procurement makes it imperative that its governments seek more cost effective procurement processes. Defense procurement remains overwhelmingly a national activity and current arrangements are expensive and inefficient, duplicating effort and raising costs. Fragmented national markets deny Europe the economies of scale necessary to reduce costs, fund R&D and ensure the effective application of technology. At the same time, these pressures are increasing not least because of the cost and complexity of those systems that are the key to military transformation.

On the supply side, the European defense industry has already undergone a dramatic consolidation, although further mergers, acquisitions and joint ventures will be necessary if industry is to address the emerging capability agenda. Equally, that capability agenda requires governments to address demand-side deficiencies. Recent political developments suggest that, at last, European governments appear serious about developing closer cooperation between themselves in the field of armaments. The most tangible sign of this new determination is the proposed European Armaments, Research and Military Capabilities Agency. Such a reform of the demand side is important and long overdue because it will help Europe procure more cost-effective, technologically-advanced and timely defense equipment.

Ultimately, however, the pace of technological developments in the United States, combined with constraints on European defense R&D and procurement budgets, mean that Europe will only meet its capabilities needs through a combination of European developments complemented by transatlantic armaments cooperation. If transatlantic cooperation is to be successful in this new environment, the U.S. needs to recognize the technological capabilities of European partners as well as the political imperative for balanced cooperative arrangements. For NATO transformation to be effective, the United States must be willing to trust its European partners by sharing advanced technology, such as stealth and command-and-control systems. Moreover, the

U.S. government will likely need to relax technology transfer and export controls if it wishes allies to have comparable capabilities. These are big challenges for policy makers and politicians on both sides of the Atlantic.

Transformation and the U.S. Defense Industry

The imbalance in European and U.S. military capabilities has been an issue for NATO throughout its history, but the last decade has seen rising concerns that this gap could grow to such an extent that U.S. and European armed forces will find it increasingly difficult to operate effectively together.[2] The U.S. focus on transformation has only heightened these concerns. The CSIS Commission on Transatlantic Security and Industrial Cooperation in the Twenty-First Century bluntly states the problem: "The Bush administration has made military transformation a central defense and national security objective and has embarked on a radical reorganization and transformation of its military resources and capabilities at a speed and of a scope that current European defense budgets are in no position to match any time soon."[3] Joint Vision 2020, like Joint Vision 2010 before it, paints a picture of a U.S. military that leverages information superiority to dominate the full spectrum of military operations, from low intensity conflict to major theater wars. The Quadrennial Defense Review (QDR) focused on dominant military capabilities that would be reinforced by a transformation in doctrine and technology and able to operate on a global basis. As Dombrowski and Ross observe: "Information superiority is to be the underpinning of 'dominant maneuver', 'precision engagement', 'focused logistics', and 'full-dimensional protection'. U.S. forces are expected to prevail over any and all military challengers by moving more quickly, hitting harder and more precisely, and when necessary, sustaining operations longer than potential adversaries."[4]

---

[2] For two competing view on the transatlantic capabilities gap see: David C. Gompert, Richard L Kugler and Martin C. Libicki, *Mind the Gap: Promoting a Transatlantic Revolution in Military Affairs*, National Defense University Press, Washington DC (1999) and Robert P. Grant, "The RMA—Europe can keep in step," Occasional Papers 15, June 2000, Western European Union Institute for Security Studies (Paris).

[3] *The Future of the Transatlantic Defense Community*, p.3.

[4] Peter J. Dombrowski and Andrew L. Ross, "Transforming the Navy: Punching a Feather Bed?," *Naval War College Review*, Vol. LVI, No.3, Summer 2003, pp.108-109.

Such concepts are being supported by a slow but perceptible redirection of R&D and procurement spending. Within the huge hike in U.S. defense R&D spending is a new Transformational Technology Initiative focusing attention on hypersonics and space access, advanced reconnaissance and knowledge architecture and power and energy technologies. Patterns of procurement spending are also changing. The cancellation of the U.S. Army's $1.1 billion Crusader artillery program is seen as evidence that transformation will have a direct impact on the future shape of U.S. defense equipment requirements.[5]

Within the U.S. Department of Defense there are those who argue that these developments require a transformation of the defense industrial base.[6] They also argue that support of "effects-based operations" means understanding the defense industrial base as being composed of operational effects-based sectors rather than platforms. Decision processes within the acquisition system should be organized to optimize operational effects rather than programs, platforms or weapons systems. At the same time, investment and sourcing of transformational technologies may require the DOD to look beyond its traditional suppliers to commercial companies and start-ups in sectors as diverse as robotics, information technology and pharmaceuticals.

Indeed, since "The Last Supper,"[7] the U.S. defense industry has been shifting the focus of its activities from platforms towards defense electronics and systems integration activities. The Bush Administration's focus on transformation has given added impetus to that process.[8] 2002 and 2003 saw a series of acquisitions of emerging

---

[5] Gopal Ratnam, "Industry considers transformation needs," *Defense News* Top 100, http://www.defensenews.com/story.php?F=1335311&C=top100

[6] *Transforming the Defense Industrial Base: A Roadmap*, Office of the Deputy Under Secretary of Defense (Industrial Policy), Department of Defense, Washington DC February 2003 http://www.acq.osd.mil/ip

[7] "The Last Supper" is a term attributed to then Lockheed Martin Chairman Norman Augustine to describe a meeting in early 1993 at which then Defense Secretary Les Aspin informed senior U.S. defense industry leaders that due to impending budget cuts and force reductions, the U.S. Department of Defense anticipated radical restructuring and consolidation of the defense industry and that the Pentagon would not intervene to prevent large mergers and acquisitions, or even liquidation, of defense companies.

[8] For a discussion of how U.S. defense industry consolidation since "The Last Supper" has caused a gradual shift from platforms towards electronics, see Andrew D. James, ""Defence industry consolidation and post-merger management: Lessons from the United States," *International Journal of Aerospace Management*, Vol.1 No.3, 2001, pp.252-267.

defense information technology companies by large defense contractors—General Dynamics' acquisition of Veridian is a prominent example of such deals.[9] General Dynamics is a striking example of how companies have reshaped their activities towards the growing defense information technology sector. Northrop Grumman and Lockheed Martin have done much the same and Boeing has recast itself from an aircraft, missiles and satellite maker to a large-scale systems integrator, capable of orchestrating the design and development of any weapon system. Thus, a team led by Boeing and Science Applications International Corp., (SAIC) San Diego, won a $5 billion contract from the U.S. Army to design its Future Combat Systems and followed that up by winning a $2 billion contract to design the Army's Joint Tactical Radio System.

Developments in Europe

While the Pentagon has pushed ahead with its transformation efforts, European governments have been more cautious, preferring evolution to revolution. In large part, this reflects the reality of European defense procurement budgets. The demands on European defense budgets stem first from the continuing need of most European countries to pursue transformation of their militaries from a Cold War posture focused on territorial defense to one that provides a substantial ability to conduct force projection operations, and second from the large costs of capabilities associated with the Revolution in Military Affairs (RMA).[10] There are major European concerns about the enormous potential cost of pursuing the U.S. vision of Network Centric Warfare (NCW). Investments in strategic air lift, C4ISR and the like represent considerable items of expenditure. Equally, the introduction of new technologies in one area may have knock-on effects in other areas. Thus, legacy platforms may need to be upgraded to ensure interoperability. This is expenditure that Europe can ill afford. The United States spends over 3 per cent of its GDP on defense and this figure is rising. By contrast, NATO Europe spends only about 2 per cent and this figure is more or less static. Furthermore, only Norway, Turkey

---

[9] "Challenges for the defence industry: implications of the Iraq War", *Strategic Comments*, Vol.9, Issue 7, 2003, International Institute for Strategic Studies (London).

[10] Grant, "The RMA—Europe can keep in step."

and the United Kingdom are spending the same proportion of their defense budgets on research, development and procurement as does the United States.[11] At the same time, a few large programs take a large share of existing modernization spending. Thus, the Eurofighter program is expected to consume over half the modernization budgets of Germany, Italy and Spain in coming years. Shifting substantial spending to meet transformational needs in the areas of advanced surveillance and precision targeting systems is likely to require difficult decisions related to force structures, the mix of platforms and enabling capabilities and the like.[12] The U.K. government, for one, has made it clear that there is no realistic way that it can—or would wish to—follow the U.S. vision of wholesale transformation of its forces. Instead, the UK is pursuing an incremental and selective development of transformational capabilities where it believes they are most likely to improve the effectiveness of British armed forces in a context of coalition warfare. The situation in France is similar.

This is not to say, however, that European governments have not recognized the importance of the U.S. doctrinal shift towards transformation and the need for investment in transformational mobility and network-centric assets. Within NATO Europe, the United Kingdom is furthest ahead in the shift towards expeditionary warfare, as an outcome of the 1998 Strategic Defense Review (SDR). The New Chapter of the Strategic Defense Review (SDR NC) published in July 2002 reinforced the growing importance of Network Enabled Capability (NEC) to the way the United Kingdom will choose to conduct future military operations.[13] The SDR NC commits to an acceleration of the process and to an increase in investment in NEC. This intent has been supported by the increase in defense spending announced as part of the Government's Spending Review 2002. The defense budget will rise by £3.5 billion between 2002/3 and 2005/6, representing 1.2 per cent average annual real growth over the three year period. Within this was some £1 billion of new capital and £1/2

---

[11] "Defence Expenditures of NATO Countries (1980—2002)", NATO Press Release M-DPC-2 (2002) 139 20 Dec. 2002 http://www.nato.int/docu/pr/2002/p02-139e.htm

[12] Assembly of Western European Union, *The Gap in Defence Research and Technology between Europe and the United States*, Report submitted on behalf of the Technological and Aerospace Committee, Forty-Sixth Session, December 6, 2000 (Paris).

[13] *The Strategic Defence Review: A New Chapter*, Ministry of Defence, Cm 5566 Vol.1, July 2002, The Stationery Office (London)

billion of new resources for the equipment and capabilities needed to respond to the additional challenges described in the SDR NC. The UK is investing in strategic air lift (leasing C-17s and ordering the A400M), strategic sea lift (entering into a Public Private Partnership arrangement to acquire roll-on, roll-off ferries); enhanced strike capabilities (the acquisition of two aircraft carriers from a BAE Systems and Thales consortium, the MBDA Storm Shadow air launched cruise missile and U.S. sea launched cruise missiles); and enhanced C4ISR capabilities (Bowman, Falcon, Cormorant, the Skynet 5 satellite communication system and the Watchkeeper UAV). At the same time, the shift towards NEC-based expeditionary warfare is leading to painful cuts in some areas. The Defence White Paper published in December 2003 will lead to deep cuts in existing UK heavy armor in favor of a family of new armored vehicles, known as FRES (Future Rapid Effects System). The Royal Navy will get its two new aircraft carriers but some of the fleet's older ships will be scrapped. The number of Eurofighters to be bought by the UK will be scaled back.[14]

In similar vein, France has announced its intention to embark on a modernization plan with a shift in strategy toward creating the capability to project military force anywhere in the world. The French government's plans for military funding between 2003 and 2008 boosts defense spending in 2003 to $13.3 billion, a $1.1 billion increase from the current level, and to $14.7 billion by 2008. The new programming law emphasizes three main areas of focus: intelligence (development of a new Syracuse satellite communications network; two new Helios II reconnaissance satellites, and projects to acquire Medium-Altitude Long- Endurance (MALE) and Multi-sensor Multi-mission (MCMM) UAVs); strike (additional Rafale combat aircraft, a new additional aircraft carrier and the A400M strategic airlifter); and, defense and protection of forces against nuclear, biological and chemical weapons.

Sweden provides a further interesting example of European-style transformation and an illustration of what is possible within even a relatively limited procurement budget. In 1999, Sweden announced the launch of "Det nya forsvaref" ("The New Defense"), a radically

---

[14] *Delivering Security in a Changing World* Defence White Paper, Presented to Parliament by the Secretary of State for Defence, CM 6040, December 2003, The Stationery Office (London).

restructured defense and security posture strongly influenced by the RMA. The New Defense will result in every Swedish weapons platform being plugged into an Internet-based command and control (C2) system by 2010 and a full operational capability is planned by 2020.[15] Sweden is developing a new command and control system—the Ledsyst—and the ambition of Swedish defense policy is to take decisive steps towards a network based defense.[16] Although most of the activity to date has been conceptual, Sweden has begun the development of demonstrators and field experimentation with Ledsyst projects designed to address novel C3I systems from the vantage point of technology, methods, personnel and organization.

The situation in other major European countries is less positive. In Germany, there has been a great deal of conceptual thinking about the implications of transformation for the Bundeswehr.[17] In October 2003, German Defense Minister Peter Struck announced what is a radical reorientation of the Bundeswehr. The consequences for procurement have yet to be spelled out but it is likely that we will see a reorientation of German procurement spending towards transformational capabilities. Several pilot projects have been launched aimed at developing and testing a wide range of potential solutions in areas such as IT security and interoperability.[18] In addition, and after lengthy political wrangling, Germany is investing in strategic airlift capabilities through the A400M program and missile defense through the MEADS program. However, Germany's defense budget crisis has limited the scope for German adoption of transformational technologies and has held back the process of force modernization. Germany was the last major country to begin restructuring its armed forces. It spends 1.5 per cent of GDP on defense, one of the lowest levels in relation to GDP in Europe, and compared to an average of 2.0 per cent for NATO Europe as a whole. There is a similar story in Italy. The government's concern

---

[15] Nick Cook, "Network-centric warfare—The new face of C41," *Interavia*, February 2001, Vol. 56 (650), pp.37-40.

[16] Martin Axelson and E. Anders Eriksson (2002) *Towards an Industry for Network Based Defence? Creating Information Age Defence Systems*, FIND Programme, FOI Swedish Defence Research Agency (Stockholm)

[17] See, for instance: "The future of Budeswehr transformation," presentation by Colonel Ralph Thiele, Commander of the Bundeswehr Center for Analyses and Studies (ZASBw) to a conference at SAIS, John Hopkins University, May 15, 2003.

[18] Axelson and Eriksson, *Towards an Industry for Network Based Defence?*, op. cit.

to reduce its technology gap with its allies is reflected in its prioritization of air defense and airborne surveillance. Airborne early warning aircraft, surface-to-air missile batteries, mobile and fixed surveillance radars and C4I have all been identified as critical areas for funding but budget problems are likely to slow progress.

The Challenges for the European Defense Industry

There is little doubt that the European defense industry faces considerable challenges in trying to keep pace with developments in the United States. The main challenge for the European defense industry has been that its principal customers—namely European governments—have been slow to adopt the new transformational technologies and allocate the budgets for procurement and R&D necessary for modernization. A report by the Assembly of Western European Union in 2000 observed that the gap in military research spending between the United States and Europe meant not only that a technological gap existed but that it would probably widen still further.[19] General Klaus Naumann, the former Chairman of NATO's Military Committee, has argued that even if there are niches in which the Europeans have the lead, they are at least five years behind the United States in the crucial area of C4I (command, control, communications, computers and intelligence).[20]

The scale of these challenges has prompted some U.S. commentators to question whether autonomous European development and acquisition efforts are necessarily the most effective means of utilizing scarce European defense spending. In the eyes of some U.S. commentators, the European defense industry has rather little to offer in closing the capabilities gap. European governments are not seen as seriously addressing the transatlantic capabilities gap nor is the European defense industrial base seen as capable of delivering needed capabilities. In this view, the U.S. drive towards transformation, along with its increasing defense spending, has given U.S. industry an already unassailable technological lead. Not only that, but the United States is said to have stronger commercial information industries than Europe and successful acquisition reform is allowing the Department

---

[19] *The Gap in Defence Research and Technology between Europe and the United States.*
[20] Ibid.

of Defense to gain access to those commercial technologies through a growing use of standard off-the-shelf products.[21] Such commentators argue that European programs that lead to a duplication of development efforts are costly and wasteful in the context of European spending constraints. The A400M and Galileo programs have been singled out for particular U.S. criticism. The naysayers concede that, selectively, the Europeans may have some excellent defense and information technologies; but overall they are lagging and will fall even further behind as U.S. industry responds to the demands of the Department of Defense's transformational agenda.[22] The United States can offer operational capabilities, whilst European projects are in many cases still on the drawing board. European collaborative efforts to catch-up with the United States—the naysayers continue—are likely to be more costly and quite possibly technologically inferior to buying off-the-shelf from the United States.

Undoubtedly, there are situations where European governments will seek to acquire U.S. technologies off-the-shelf. Such arrangements have a long history dating back to the F-16 program and earlier. In the 1980s, the United Kingdom and France both decided to acquire the Boeing E3 AWACS (Airborne Warning and Control System) in recognition of the fact that it was neither technologically feasible nor cost effective to seek to develop a similar capability.[23] In 1995, and for similar reasons, France ordered the E2-C Hawkeye airborne early warning/command and control aircraft for the French Navy. More recently, the UK government has made clear its view that the technologies that underpin the RMA "will inevitably be led by the U.S."[24] Thus, the UK needs to be selective about the technologies it develops nationally or on a European basis, and should be prepared to use U.S. technologies in other areas in order to continue to make a leading contribution to multinational operations. Accordingly, the UK government has selected Raytheon-developed technology to meet its Astor airborne ground surveillance requirement; looked to the

---

[21] Gompert et al, *Mind the Gap.*

[22] Paul Mann, "Technology gap called NATO's salient issue," *Aviation Week & Space Technology,* June 17, 1995; David C. Gompert et al, note 2.

[23] The U.K. had attempted to do so with its Nimrod AEW program but that was eventually cancelled due to technological difficulties and massive cost overruns

[24] Strategic Defence Review, "Supporting Essay Three, The Impact of Technology," Para.32.

Canadian subsidiary of General Dynamics for its Bowman communications program; and, is currently evaluating the acquisition of the Cooperative Engagement Capability as the basis for its naval network-centric warfare capability.

However, the acquisition of U.S. technology remains an unattractive option for many European governments. There is a strong feeling in Europe that it is crucially important to the development of ESDP that Europe establish a strong and competitive defense industrial and technological base. In this view, autonomous crisis-management operations are feasible only if Europeans succeed in narrowing the technological gap that exists between European countries and the United States and Europe must do so either through its own efforts or as an equal partner in transatlantic cooperative programs.[25] European governments are wary of the operational constraints that can emerge from U.S. technology controls, and even America's closest European allies are concerned about the need to retain an independent capability while ensuring coherence with U.S. developments. Thus, the challenge for the UK is how to achieve interoperability without being obliged to buy U.S. equipment with all the technology transfer and operational challenges that it entails.[26] At the same time, the politics of defense procurement means that politicians will continue to demand local content in exchange for their agreement to spend large sums on defense equipment and—in the current climate of weak electoral support for defense spending in Europe—initiatives that oblige European governments to buy U.S. technology are unlikely to gain much support.

Strengthening the European Defense Industry

European industry has already gone some way to establishing European solutions to European capability shortfalls. In the area of precision strike weapons, the European missile company MBDA has developed the Storm Shadow/Scalp EG cruise missile. In C4ISR, France is deploying the Helios series of optical observation satellites. A European industry team offered the Stand Off Surveillance and Target Acquisition Radar (Sostar) as an alternative to the Northrop Grumman

---

[25] *The Gap in Defence Research and Technology between Europe and the United States.*

[26] Andrew D. James, *Delivering Network Enabled Capability: Industrial, Procurement & Policy Challenges for the UK*, FIND User Report, FOI, Stockholm (forthcoming).

J-Stars for the NATO Air Ground Surveillance (AGS) requirement.[27] Similarly, Europe has programs that span the entire spectrum of Unmanned Aerial Vehicles (UAVs) and the French companies Sagem and Dassault Aviation are collaborating to develop an unmanned combat air vehicle (UCAV).[28] Europe can more than hold its own in conventional platforms and this is reflected in European technological capabilities related to strategic mobility assets. Thus, with respect to air-to-air refuelling, the Air Tanker consortium led by the European Aeronautic Defense & Space Company (EADS) is offering the A330 for the United Kingdom's Future Strategic Tanker aircraft program and the A310 Multi Role Tanker Transport aircraft has been ordered by Germany. The Airbus Military Company A400M represents a European industrial response to NATO Europe's strategic airlift needs.

The development of strong capabilities in transformational technologies is seen by European industry as vital to sustain the European defense industrial base and retain Europe's established defense export markets. European companies are also keen to gain a substantial share in the significant growth market for C4ISR, UAVs and so forth. Like their U.S. counterparts, the leading European defense contractors are responding to the new transformational agenda albeit in a way that reflects the realities of European defense budgets and the demands of their customers. BAE Systems is investing considerable effort in the development of a C4ISTAR sector strategy to address key programs in the United States, the United Kingdom and the rest of the world by building on capabilities in BAE North America (not least in the areas of Electronic Warfare and Information Dominance) and focusing across the organization to exploit technological capabilities and market opportunities.[29] As part of this strategy, BAE Systems and Italy's Finmeccanica are to form a new defense electronics partnership, to be called Eurosystems, that will oversee joint ventures in the areas of systems integration and C4ISR business, communications systems and

---

[27] SOSTAR is being developed by Thales, the Dornier unit of EADS, Alenia Difesa's FIAR and the Dutch government-owned Technisch Natuurwetenschappelyk (Luke Hill, "NATO considers merging ags," *Jane's Defence Weekly*, June 13, 2001, p.3).

[28] John Brosky, "French flying fast to win share in UCAV market," *Defense News*, April 29-May 5 2002, p.8.

[29] BAE Systems presentation by John Weston, Chief Executive at the CSFB/Aviation Week Aerospace Finance Conference, New York, May 15, 2001 downloaded April 24, 2003 from http//:www.production.investis.com/baesystems/bae_irpresentations/ csfbwebcast/2.pdf

avionics. BAE Systems is not alone. Thales is re-orientating its communications business group to focus on network-centric warfare and to capitalize on its strong position in the defense electronics business and its place as the largest European supplier of defense communication systems.[30] EADS is seeking to focus on growth areas of the global defense market such as UAVs, C4ISR and avionics. EADS has sought to use acquisitions to overcome the constraints of small defense electronics business and limited global presence outside its home markets of France, Germany and Spain. In July 2001, EADS acquired Cogent Defense & Security Networks from Nortel Networks, establishing EADS Telecom as a significant competitor in defense communications. In May 2003, EADS completed the acquisition of the BAE System share in the Astrium space joint venture and with it took full control of Paradigm Secure Communications, making EADS the prime contractor for the U.K.'s Skynet 5 program.

Ultimately, however, the European defense industry is hamstrung by the nature of the European defense market. Defense procurement remains overwhelmingly a national activity and the current arrangements are expensive and inefficient, duplicating effort and raising costs. Fragmented national markets deny Europe the economies of scale necessary to reduce costs, fund R&D and ensure the effective application of technology. National procurement requirements differ, making it difficult for companies to plan for the long-term through industry restructuring, alliance building and R&D investment. Industry figures in Europe have repeatedly warned that Europe's defense technological position relative to the United States is at risk of erosion without significant increases in European defense spending for research, development and for the procurement of advanced weapons systems.[31]

Enhancing European Armaments Cooperation

A key challenge is to develop effective models for European armaments cooperation: identifying common requirements; promoting R&T cooperation; and, improving program management.

---

[30] Gopal Ratnam and Amy Svitak, "How Europe can close the gap," *Defense News*, August 5-11 2002, pp.1-4.

[31] "Hertrich: Europe's defense technology future at risk absent more funding," *Defense Daily International*, February 15, 2002.

Transformation will amplify the need for international co-operation at defense industry level, in order to make best use of scarce skilled resources and finite communications capacity, and to meet the need to network with coalition partners.[32] Many European countries are currently studying and undertaking network related/network centric warfare developments and there is considerable opportunity to share research, leverage experimentation and build coalition capability.[33] The UK government has made it clear that it is willing to consider international collaboration in the development of such capabilities. In the case of FIST (the U.K.'s future soldier technology program), the Defense Procurement Agency notes that many NATO and Partnership for Peace nations are pursuing similar programs and the FIST Assessment Phase is looking carefully at collaborative opportunities. The French government has also expressed its desire to increase its cooperative R&D effort and has argued that across a range of transformational technology areas from space to C4ISR there is a strong case for European solutions.[34]

Historically, collaborative equipment programs among European nations have proved highly problematic. Where European governments have decided to pursue collaborative programs, those programs have all too often been based on strict *juste retour* work share agreements to satisfy national governments' needs to deliver local jobs in exchange for spending taxpayers' money on defense. At the same time, these collaborative programs have frequently been dogged by problems because they have often been established after national equipment requirements have become relatively firm—leaving the collaborative program to try to deliver a common solution to often-conflicting national requirements. The consequence has been a high failure rate amongst such programs and cost over-runs for those that have survived.

The A400M debacle is a good example of much that shackles Europe in delivering conventional capabilities. The Airbus Military

---

[32] *Defence Industrial Policy*, Paper No.5, Ministry of Defence Policy Papers, October 2002, Ministry of Defence (London).

[33] *Network Enabled Capability: The UK's programme to enhance military capability by better exploitation of information*, downloaded April 24, 2003 from http://www.mod.uk/issues/nec/

[34] *Rapport fait au nom de la Commission de la Défense Nationale et des Forces Armees sur le project de loi (no.187) relative a la programmation militaire por les années 2003 à 2008*, M. Guy Teissier, November 25, 2002, Assemblée Nationale (Paris).

Company A-400M is a critical part of the European Union's plans to set up an autonomous Rapid Reaction Force because the aircraft is intended to provide Europe with an indigenous medium- to heavy-lift military transport aircraft. Eight countries—Belgium, France, Germany, Luxembourg, Portugal, Spain, Turkey and the United Kingdom—plan to procure the A400M. The eight nations plan to order a total of 196 aircraft and the program will be managed by the European program management organization OCCAR (Organization for Joint Armaments Cooperation). However, even though there is a consensus among European governments to improve their collective airlift capability, getting the joint program under way has been difficult. One of the main challenges has been to get all the participants to maintain their procurement commitments. Italy has withdrawn from the program, and internal political and funding problems have meant that German's commitment to the program has been brought into question on several occasions before it finally confirmed its orders.[35]

ETAP (European Technology Acquisition Program) is another example of the challenges of inter-governmental cooperation. ETAP was established in 2001 to develop future European combat aircraft and UCAV capabilities. It comprises France, Germany, Italy, Spain, Sweden and the U.K. together with the leading European defense companies. ETAP is designed to lay the foundations for European combat air systems of the future. Future combat air systems may include manned aircraft (which may well be developments of existing aircraft such as Eurofighter, Gripen and Rafale); air and ground launched UAVs and UCAVs; conventionally-armed long-range cruise missiles (CALCM); and command, control, communication, computing, and intelligence (C4I) systems to link all these together.[36] However, progress has been slow not least because of political disputes over the focus of the program and a U.K.-French dispute over stealth technology.

---

[35] Katia Vlachos-Dengler, *From National Champions to European Heavyweights: The Development of European Defense Industrial Capabilities across Market Segments*, RAND National Defense Research Institute (Santa Monica), 2002.

[36] "European governments and industry to cooperate on future capabilities and technologies for combat air systems," Press notice on behalf of the defense ministries of France, Germany, Italy, Spain, Sweden and the United Kingdom, November 19, 2001, Paris.

Nonetheless, European governments are seeking to make progress and to observers of European armaments cooperation recent political developments have been nothing short of remarkable. The idea of a European armaments agency, having languished for more than a decade, has reemerged on to the political agenda and European governments appear serious about developing closer cooperation in the field of armaments. The Anglo-French Le Touquet Declaration, the draft Constitutional Treaty produced by the Convention on the Future of Europe and the conclusions of the Thessalonki European Council all suggest the emergence of a new political dynamic to the process that seemed inconceivable only a few years ago. The draft Constitutional Treaty included a proposal to establish an intergovernmental European Armaments, Research and Military Capabilities Agency that would identify operational requirements, put forward measures to satisfy those requirements, contribute to identifying and implementing measures needed to strengthen the European defense industrial and technological base, participate in defining a European capabilities and armaments policy, and assist the Council in evaluating the improvement of military capabilities.[37] In October 2003, European defense ministers agreed to further and substantially harmonize their armed forces by the end of the decade. Meeting informally in Rome, ministers agreed to significantly increase their interoperability by 2010, pooling resources, doctrines and equipment to ensure they are able to "work seamlessly together and with key strategic partners."[38] The agreement sets a new deadline for military cooperation just months before the end of the 2003 deadline for the Helsinki Headline Goal.

The political attention being given to armaments cooperation is encouraging, but a moment's reflection on the history of European armaments cooperation reminds us that we have been down this road before, only for it to end with little in the way of concrete developments. The character of European armaments cooperation has been determined by the desire of national governments to protect national sovereignty and control over armaments issues, combined with the unbridgeable gap between the interests of large and small European

---

[37] Draft Constitution, Volume I, CONV 724/03, Secretariat of the European Convention, Brussels, May 26, 2003.

[38] Statement by Javier Solana, Rome October 3-4, 2003. http://ue.eu.int/newsroom/new-main.asp?LANG=1

countries. Those European countries with large defense industrial bases have favored intergovernmental coalitions of the willing such as OCCAR and the Framework Agreement as a means of achieving some progress on armaments cooperation issues. Turning the grand political statements of support for a European armaments agency into real progress may prove to be far from straightforward, and the road ahead may be a rocky one. Indeed, the history of European armaments cooperation has been one of often torturous negotiations over the minutiae of implementation that have had the effect of eroding the dynamic created by high-level political initiatives. Important issues still have to be addressed: the integration of existing armaments cooperation organizations; the membership of the Agency and the possibility of enhanced cooperation; the responsibilities of the Agency and the willingness of national governments to provide it with the necessary executive powers; concerns about European preference; and the role of the European Commission.

At the same time, European policy makers must make sure that this latest round of institution-building does not lead them to lose sight of the bigger picture. The Agency should not be seen as end in itself. Success will be measured not by the establishment of the institution (we have had plenty of those in the last three decades) but by the difference that it makes to European capabilities in support of ESDP. In this regard, the Agency can be regarded as a necessary but not a sufficient condition for progress towards meeting Europe's aspirations. The political will to address the capabilities issue expressed in the ECAP process and now in thinking about the Agency is encouraging. Ultimately, however, the Agency will only deliver results if it is supported by the will to increase European defense procurement spending to a level that ensures that European military forces can meet the political aspirations of the ESDP and NATO transformation.

Promoting Transatlantic Cooperation

However, the pace of technological developments in the United States, combined with constraints on European defense R&D and procurement budgets, mean that Europe will only meet its capabilities needs through a combination of European developments complemented by transatlantic armaments cooperation. The CSIS Commission on Transatlantic Security and Industrial Cooperation in the

Twenty-First Century argues convincingly: "Both NATO and the European Union should make an effort to coordinate on defining priority defense requirements and equipment needs that could be met by consortia or partnerships among industrial suppliers and technology companies across the Atlantic."[39] Cooperation on missile defense and unmanned aerial vehicles are two significant areas where coordination could avoid redundant spending and there are benefits for both sides. The CSIS report observes that: "U.S. military capabilities could take advantage of technologies that are being developed in Europe, while the Europeans could achieve more effective technological pooling with U.S. defense capabilities, reinforcing progress towards coalition interoperability."[40] The outcome could well be NATO-owned and operated assets such as NATO AWACS or capabilities that could be adopted by individual member states. Such arrangements offer the prospect of reducing problems of interoperability and enhancing NATO military capabilities.

Currently, the degree of cooperative engagement in armaments development and production is extremely low. Significantly, there is virtually no meaningful cooperative engagement in key U.S. transformation programs—from UAVs to military space to information dominance—or in the other areas that are relevant to closing the capability gap or enhancing interoperability. Current transatlantic cooperative efforts are, by and large, not related to coalition force improvements in interoperability or capability, but undertaken for reasons of affordability (JSF) and geopolitics (missile defense).[41]

Of course, the record of transatlantic armaments cooperation has been patchy. There have been some success stories. The long term multi-national Sea Sparrow and Evolved Sea Sparrow Missile (ESSM) program could be cited as an example of how joint cooperative programs could be put together to allow for both commonality and economic participation.[42] The Joint Tactical Information & Distribution System (JTIDS) program has enhanced interoperability between NATO combat aircraft. However, the story of the NATO Air Ground

---

[39] *The Future of the Transatlantic Defense Community*, p.ix.

[40] *The Future of the Transatlantic Defense Community*, p.11

[41] *The Future of the Transatlantic Defense Community*, p.11

[42] *Trans-Atlantic Defence Industrial Cooperation*, A report by the NATO Industrial Advisory Group to the Conference of National Armaments Directors, Spring 2002, Brussels.

Surveillance system (AGS) is a sobering reminder of the challenge of turning warm words into concrete action. The AGS project has been beset by political and industrial difficulties. U.S. proposals based around its Multi-Platform Radar Technology Insertion Program (MP-RTIP) initially proved problematic because key areas of classified technology were offered on a "black-box" basis only. At the political level, 2001 saw France, Germany, Italy, Spain and the Netherlands attempting to secure their own technology base by supporting a research program dubbed Stand-Off Surveillance and Target Acquisition Radar (Sostar) to develop an active-phased array SAR/MTI radar. Northrop Grumman is the U.S. prime on MP-RTIP, while EADS is a major partner in Sostar. However, both companies are also exploring a number of areas of transatlantic collaboration, which has given rise to the Transatlantic Industrial Proposal Solution (TIPS) to meet the NATO AGS, while also aiming to placate political concerns in both Europe and the U.S.[43] Joint Strike Fighter—for many a model for the future of transatlantic armaments cooperation—has struggled to overcome the challenges of U.S. arms export and technology transfer regulations.

Transformation-oriented cooperative armaments programs (or European participation in ongoing U.S. programs) may provide a means of closing the capabilities gap. Equally, deep and balanced transatlantic links between defense research agencies in the United States and Europe could help so long as they go beyond the current exchange of information to incorporate joint projects.[44] To facilitate such common programs requires agreement on operational requirements, and new and more efficient ways of managing projects collaboratively. NATO members also need to coordinate acquisition purchases to achieve economies of scale. Such cooperation needs to recognize the technological capabilities of European partners as well as the political imperative for balanced cooperative arrangements and can only be built on a willingness to draw on component technologies from participating nations in a fair manner. This means paying more attention to operational requirements, willingness to invest, capabilities, and efficiency than national origin and offset arrangements.[45]

---

[43] Douglas Barrie and Michael A. Taverna, "Prague Summit Could Provide Springboard for NATO AGS", *Aviation Week & Space Technology*, July 8 2002, Vol. 157 (2), p. 31.

[44] The Gap in Defence Research and Technology between Europe and the United States.

[45] *The Future of the Transatlantic Defense Community*, p.x

Creating a Transatlantic Defense Industry

Another way in which the U.S. and European governments could promote transatlantic cooperation is through support for transatlantic defense industrial linkages and joint ventures.[46] European defense companies are already pursuing industrial relationships with U.S. companies as a means of accessing U.S. technology and filling their own capability gaps. Of course, further industrial linkages will only emerge if they make commercial sense to defense contractors. Thus, programs like NATO AGS have a potentially critical role in providing a focus for transatlantic teaming not least because new technologies and opportunities for change can be created by nurturing multiple partnerships among prime contractors.[47] Equally, governments on both sides of the Atlantic need to sustain and enhance the climate for transatlantic teaming, joint ventures and M&A through periodic affirmation that such forms of transatlantic industrial cooperation are desired.

There has been some progress. One notable transatlantic defense industrial development is the strategic alliance between EADS and Northrop Grumman. The two companies signed a Memorandum of Understanding in 2001 under which they agreed to explore opportunities in ground surveillance and a number of other areas of defense electronics, such as aerial targets and decoys, airborne electronic attack and fire control radar. The first product of this relationship was an agreement to offer a 'European version' of a weather and navigation radar, developed by Northrop Grumman, for the Airbus A400M military transport aircraft.[48] A further development has been the agreement between Northrop Grumman and EADS to develop a Eurohawk variant of Northrop Grumman's Global Hawk UAV for marketing in Europe. The most substantial part of the two companies' common activities is their collaboration on NATO AGS.

Equally significant is the joint venture between Thales and Raytheon. Thales Raytheon Systems Company has combined the

---

[46] Robert Hunter, George Joulwan and C. Richard Nelson, *New Capabilities: Transforming NATO Forces*, The Atlantic Council of the United States, Washington D.C. (September 2002).

[47] Robbin Laird, "Industry transformation: company efforts can help reshape military," *Defense News*, May 6-12 2002, p.13.

[48] John D. Morrocco, 'EADS, Northrop Grumman broaden cooperative links,' *Aviation Week & Space Technology*, June 12, 2000, pp. 35-6.

capabilities of the two companies in the area of air defense command and control centers, air defense radars and battlefield air surveillance in North America.

More significant still, from the point of view of transatlantic defense industrial relationships, have been the acquisitions undertaken by BAE Systems in the United States. BAE Systems North America Inc. is now one of the leading suppliers to the U.S. Department of Defense as a consequence of its acquisition of Lockheed Martin's Aerospace Systems and Electronic Systems businesses and its earlier acquisition of Sanders (as part of GEC Marconi). These acquisitions have given BAE Systems a leading position in the growing U.S. market and they also present the opportunity for BAE Systems to gain access to U.S. R&D programs and technology. A key element of BAE Systems' C4ISTAR sector strategy is to build on its North American capabilities in EW and information dominance and leverage them into U.K. and rest of the world programs. Nevertheless, BAE Systems must contend with the constraints imposed by U.S. export and technology transfer regulations as it tries to create a true multinational business organization, and these are undoubtedly constraining its ability to utilize U.S. technology in European programs.

A Renewed U.S. Commitment to Transatlantic Armaments Cooperation

Creating the conditions for transatlantic armaments cooperation places responsibilities on both Europe and the United States. Europe needs to take the capabilities gap seriously and ensure that it reallocates scarce defense budgets to address NATO capabilities requirements. The U.S. government needs to play its part in the modernization of NATO Europe's capabilities, not least by offering technology and joint programs to support European transformation and enabling this process through changes to U.S. export and technology transfer regulations.

The reform of U.S. export and technology transfer controls is critical. U.S. arms export controls have long hampered transatlantic armaments cooperation. A major challenge for the European defense industry has been how to enter into effective collaborative ventures to acquire U.S. technology. In large part this is a function of the difficulties posed by U.S. export controls and technology transfer regulations. Time and again, these security regulations have made transatlantic collaboration difficult and—in some cases—they have driven European companies to deliberately design-out components and subsystems from European programs.

The history of the Medium Extended Air Defense System (MEADS) program highlights the sensitivity of technology transfer issues in transatlantic industrial relationships as well as the often limited political commitment to these kinds of government-to-government collaborative programs on the part of the U.S. Congress. The United States insisted on having the right to conduct on-site security inspections of German and Italian facilities, and at the same time proposed the use of 'black boxes' to protect U.S. technology. Such proposals were rejected by the German government, which saw MEADS as a test case for U.S. willingness to share technology with its allies. A stalemate ensued which was only broken after eight months of sometimes tense negotiations.[49] Similar challenges have been faced by the Joint Strike Fighter program. The UK government and industry has warned on several occasions that the JSF is in danger of foundering if technology is not approved for release. These problems have occurred despite the use of an innovative Global Project License designed to ease technology transfer between JSF program partners.[50]

There are signs of some progress. In Autumn 2002, the State Department began a review of the current policy guiding conventional arms transfers in a move that may lead to the relaxation of export regulations and that may facilitate armaments and industrial cooperation.[51] The ongoing review under the National Security Policy Directive on Defense Trade Export Policy and National Security (NSPD-19) is the latest effort to reform the U.S. export control system. As one State Department official has noted, since the 1990s there has been a growing concern that the U.S. licensing process is overly complex and slow, and increasingly incompatible with the growing trend towards multinational collaboration in the defense industry.

---

[49] Andrew D. James, "The prospects for the future", in Burkard Schmitt (ed.) *Between Cooperation and Competition: the Transatlantic Relationship*, Chaillot Paper 44, 2001, Paris.

[50] David Mulholland, "UK and US export-control disarray worsening", Jane's Defence Weekly, 26 November 2003, pp.24-25.

[51] Jason Sherman, "Reviewing U.S. export rules", *Defense News*, July 22-28 2002, p.8.

Equally, there has also been recognition within successive Administrations that the way that U.S. defense technology controls operates means that U.S. security interests were being achieved at a high cost in terms of damaged political influence and goodwill among NATO allies. At the same time, the Administration has argued that there is a direct connection with NATO transformation and reform is vital to ensure that the U.S. and its allies are able to make optimal use of advanced defense technology.[52]

Previous experience of U.S. export control reform initiatives, however, means that Europeans remain skeptical. A series of initiatives begun under the Clinton Administration made slow progress and generated considerable frustration for the countries involved. The U.S.-UK "Declaration of Principles," signed in February 2000, sought to provide a bilateral model for the management of transatlantic relationships covering the harmonization of military requirements; export procedures, information and technology-related security as well as joint research programs. The U.S. Defense Trade Security Initiative (DTSI), announced in May 2000, promised a series of actions, including streamlined program and project licenses, a review of the U.S. Munitions List, and an offer to negotiate ITAR exemption arrangements with Australia and the United Kingdom. The UK experience has been that tangible progress can be slow—it took two years before the United Kingdom introduced the first legislation. The frustrations of those involved were such that the UK minister for defense procurement, Lord Bach, was moved to complain publicly about the slow progress, describing many of the U.S.-imposed constraints on Anglo-American defense-industrial relations as "absurd."[53] Industry has been encouraged by initiatives such as DTSI and the Framework Agreement, but is withholding judgment until it sees how the outcomes of the NSPD-19 review are implemented toward a regulatory regime that is designed for better cooperation.[54] However, the climate

---

[52] "Status of U.S. Interagency Review of U.S. Export Licensing and Technology Transfer Policy", speech by Lincoln P. Bloomfield, Jr., Assistant Secretary for Political-Military Affairs, U.S. Department of State, to a conference on "Transatlantic Defense Industrial Cooperation: Challenges and Prospects" Co-sponsored by NATO and the Transatlantic Center of the German Marshall Fund of the United States, Brussels, July 18, 2003.

[53] "ITAR Waivering U.K. government presses U.S. administration to move ahead on defense reform", Aviation Week & Space Technology, May 12, 2003, p. 28.

[54] *Trans-Atlantic Defence Industrial Cooperation.*

is hardly helped by Congressional support for strengthened "Buy American" provisions and Europeans wait to see how willing the Bush Administration will be to push for change in the face of likely Congressional opposition.

This is critical because for NATO transformation to be effective, the United States must be willing to trust its European partners by sharing advanced technology, such as stealth and command-and-control systems. If the U.S. wishes its allies to have comparable capabilities then it needs to offer technology to support European transformation and promote common, joint programs to strengthen the NATO defense technological and industrial bases.[55] Cooperative Engagement Capability (CEC) is a good illustration of the difficulties. The U.S. has agreed to release CEC to the United Kingdom but given the clear advantages of the system, particularly in the interoperability arena, extending CEC across the whole of NATO would seem to be a highly desirable step. Since Norway and Spain have acquired Aegis-based naval air defense systems, they would be the obvious next recipients of CEC. What remains to be seen is how long they will have to wait for it. CEC gives the U.S. a quantum leap in its ability to achieve `full spectrum dominance' in any theatre of war and the Pentagon is reluctant to see it proliferate elsewhere. It is this aspect of CEC that makes it a curiously paradoxical program. On the one hand, it clearly represents the strongest emergent technology around for removing barriers to full transatlantic interoperability. Yet, on the other, it is too sensitive, too great a leap forward, to be given an unequivocal export release.[56] Against this background, it is little wonder that Thales has called on the French government to fund a naval net-centric system demonstrator as the basis for a European alternative to CEC. Such a development would lead to yet further duplication and stretch already over-committed European defense budgets—but it would be completely understandable nonetheless.

---

[55] Jeffrey P. Bialos, "Thoughts before yet another NATO Summit—Will Prague 'Visions' of coalition warfighting capabilities translate into armaments realities?", mimeo, The Johns Hopkins SAIS Center for Transatlantic Relations, Washington DC (September 2002).

[56] Cook, "Network-centric warfare."

Conclusion

This chapter has argued that there is a pressing need to broaden and deepen armaments cooperation, both within Europe and across the Atlantic, if NATO's transformation agenda is to deliver. Europe needs to build "Towers of Excellence" in those capability areas that are critical to its NATO commitments and the implementation of the ESDP. A strengthened European technological and industrial base is also the most likely way of strengthening transatlantic armaments cooperation. By enhancing its defense industrial capabilities, Europe is more likely to be taken seriously in Washington policy circles. Ultimately, European governments will need to selectively acquire U.S. technologies because European defense R&D and procurement budgets will make it impossible to keep pace with U.S. technological developments across the full range of capabilities. However, stronger European defense technological capabilities will give Europe more leverage at the negotiating table and is the best way to ensure that future transatlantic armaments cooperation is balanced and in European interests.

This presents major challenges to European policy makers. European industry has gone a considerable way towards cross-border consolidation. The challenge is now with European governments to find new ways to enhance intergovernmental cooperation and strengthen European capabilities. The planned European Armaments, Research and Military Capabilities Agency is a step in the right direction but the final outcome of this initiative is far from certain. The new Agency will only make a difference if it provides a platform for requirements harmonization, closer cooperation on research and armaments programs and defining a true European capabilities and armaments policy. The political will to address the capabilities issue expressed first in the ECAP process and now in thinking about the Agency is encouraging. Ultimately, however, the Agency will only deliver results if it is supported by the will to increase European defense procurement spending to a level that ensures that European military forces can meet the political aspirations of the ESDP and NATO transformation. This remains a massive challenge.

How should U.S. policy makers respond to these efforts to strengthen European capabilities? All too often Europeans feel that they face a "damned-if-you-do-damned-if-you-don't" problem. U.S.

politicians and policy makers have been keen to criticize Europeans for not doing enough or spending enough. However, when Europeans try to remedy these shortcomings and seek solutions to European capability shortfalls, they are often criticized for "duplicating" efforts and "wasting" money (the Meteor missile, A400M transport aircraft and Galileo are but three prominent examples). There is little point in the U.S. continuing to push the idea that the only solution is for Europe to "buy American." Such an idea will always be a non-starter. Instead, U.S. policy makers need to find ways of encouraging transatlantic solutions to transformational capability requirements. Joint programs in transformational technology areas need to be established and they must be supported by reform of U.S. technology transfer and arms export regulations. All too often, transatlantic programs like MEADS have been stymied by a combination of technology transfer blockages, hostility within the military services and limited Congressional support. The experience of transatlantic programs has led too many Europeans to conclude that the United States is an unreliable partner and has driven them to find alternative Europe-only solutions to their armaments requirements.

Reform efforts are under way, not least NSPD-19, and they need to be encouraged. Nevertheless, Europeans remain uncertain about U.S. commitment to transatlantic armaments cooperation. They perceive Congress to be hostile to transatlantic cooperation and wonder whether reform has the wholehearted commitment of the Bush Administration. They sense a view in some Washington circles that the U.S. has rather little to gain from transatlantic armaments cooperation because the drive towards transformation, along with increasing U.S. R&D and procurement spending, has given the U.S. an already unassailable technological lead. This leaves us to ponder what European governments and industry should do if the United States continues to be an unreliable partner in transatlantic cooperation. The answer will differ between countries. There is little doubt that the UK government and industry has a preferential position and will continue to do its best to strengthen transatlantic armaments cooperation. Italy is likely to do the same. The situation in some other leading European countries is less positive and the momentum for European preference is growing.

The Istanbul Summit presents an opportunity to move the transatlantic armaments agenda forward a few paces. The Summit should be used to reaffirm the commitment of all NATO member states to transatlantic armaments cooperation. The Summit should identify new programs in transformational technology areas that could provide the basis for future cooperation. The Summit should make a commitment to establish a standing conference on transatlantic armaments, export control and technology transfer issues that could provide a forum for high level dialogue between policy makers, politicians and defense industry representatives. This could complement the work of the Conference of National Armaments Directors (CNAD).

Should the U.S. care about transatlantic armaments cooperation? If the U.S, is serious about NATO and its transformation then the answer has to be "yes". Abandoning transatlantic armaments cooperation, either by commission or omission, will leave both the U.S. and Europe worse off. The benefits for the U.S. remain clear. Transatlantic armaments cooperation is a powerful tool to promote interoperability. The U.S. does not have a monopoly in advanced technology and Europe has important capabilities that can be of benefit to U.S. programs. Within NATO, a combination of strong European efforts complemented by transatlantic armaments cooperation can help tackle the worst of the capabilities gaps. The need for such efforts is increasingly pressing. Without new initiatives, Europe's capability shortfalls will make increasingly meaningless its political and military aspirations both within NATO and the ESDP. Within NATO, the capabilities gap is likely to lead to an ever greater divergence of doctrines between NATO Europe and the United States, making coalition warfare increasingly difficult if not impossible for all but a few European militaries. Within the European Union, the consequence could well be the emergence of an equally divisive capabilities gap between those European countries that have invested in transformational and network centric capabilities (in particular the UK and France) and the rest.

Acronyms

ACE	Allied Command Europe
ACO	Allied Command Operations
ACT	Allied Command Transformation
AGS	Air Ground Surveillance
AMF	Allied Command Europe Mobile Force
ARRC	Allied Command Europe Rapid Reaction Corps
ATMS	Army Tactical Missile System
AWACS	Airborne Warning and Control System
BRAC	Base Re-Alignment and Closing
C2	Command, Control
C3I	Command, Control, Communications and Intelligence
C4	Command, Control, Communications, Computers
C4I	Command, Control, Communications, Computers and Intelligence
C4ISR	Command, Control, Communications, Computers, Intelligence, Surveillance and Reconnaissance
CALCM	Conventionally Armed Long-range Cruise Missile
CD&E	Concept Development and Experimentation
CEC	Cooperative Engagement Capability
CFSP	Common Foreign and Security Policy
CNAD	Conference of National Armaments Directors
CPCO	*Centre de Planification et de Conduite des Operations*
CPM	Customer, Product, Management
CSIS	Center for Strategic and International Studies
DCI	Defense Capabilities Initiative
DOD	United States Department of Defense
DOPS	Declaration of Principles
DPC	Defense Planning Committee
DRR	Defense Requirements Review
DRC	Democratic Republic of Congo
DSACEUR	Deputy Supreme Allied Commander Europe
DTSI	Defense Trade Security Initiative
EADS	European Aeronautic Defense & Space Company
ECAP	European Capabilities Action Plan
EMA	*Etat-Major des Armées*
EOC	Essential Operational Capabilities

ESDP	European Security and Defense Policy
ETAP	European Technology Acquisition Program
EU	European Union
ERRF	European Rapid Reaction Force
ESDI	European Security and Defense Identity
ESDP	European Security and Defense Policy
ESSM	Evolved Sea Sparrow Missile
EW	Electronic Warfare
FIST	Future Infantry Soldier Technology
FYDP	Future Year Defense Program
FRES	Future Rapid Effects System
FRG	Federal Republic of Germany
GDP	Gross Domestic Product
GDR	German Democratic Republic
GLCM	Ground Launched Cruise Missiles
HQ	Headquarters
HRF	High Readiness Force
KFOR	Kosovo Force
HUMINT	Human Intelligence
ISAF	International Security Assistance Force
ITAR	International Traffic in Arms Regulations
JCS	Joint Chiefs of Staff
JFC	Joint Force Command
JSF	Joint Strike Fighter
JTIDS	Joint Tactical Information & Distribution System
LO/CLO	Low Observable/Counter Low Observable
LOE	Limited Objective Experiment
LTDP	Long-Term Defense Plan
M&A	Mergers & Acquisitions
MAPE	Multinational Advisory Police Element
MALE	Medium-Altitude Long-Endurance
MCMM	Multi-Sensor Multi-Mission
MEADS	Medium Extended Air Defense System
MIC	Multinational Interoperability Council
MID	Multifunctional Information Distribution System
MLRS	Multiple Launch Rocket System
MNE	Multinational Experiment
MNJCD&E	Multinational Joint Concept Development and Experimentation

MP-RTIP	Multi-Platform Radar Technology Insertion Program
NAC	North Atlantic Council
NATO	North Atlantic Treaty Organization
NBC	Nuclear-Biological-Chemical
NCW	Network Centric Warfare
NEC	Network Enabled Capability
NRF	NATO Response Force
NSPD	National Security Policy Directive
OCCAR	Organization for Joint Armaments Cooperation
PCC	Prague Capabilities Commitment
PFC	Partnership for Cooperation
PFP	Partnership for Peace
PKK	Partiya Karkeren Kurdistan (*Kurdistan Workers' Party*)
POM	Programs Objectives Memorandum
PSC	Political and Security Committee
QDR	Quadrennial Defense Review
R&D	Research and Development
RDO	Rapid Decisive Operation
RMA	Revolution in Military Affairs
RPV	Remotely Piloted Vehicles
R&T	Research and Technology
SACEUR	Supreme Allied Commander Europe
SACLANT	Supreme Allied Commander Atlantic
SAC-T	Supreme Allied Commander, Transformation
SAIC	Science Applications International Corp.
SAR/MTI	Synthetic Aperture Radar and Moving Target Indicator
SASPF	Standard Application Software Product Family
SDR	Strategic Defense Review
SDR NC	New Chapter of the Strategic Defense Review
SEAD	Suppression of Enemy Air Defenses
SHAPE	Supreme Headquarters Allied Powers in Europe
SJFHQ	Standing Joint Forces Headquarters
SFOR	Stabilization Force
SOF	Special Operation Forces
S&R	Stabilization & Reconstruction
SOSTAR	Stand-Off Surveillance and Target Acquisition Radar
TIPS	Transatlantic Industrial Proposal Solution
UAV	Unmanned Aerial Vehicles

UCAV	Unmanned Combat Aerial Vehicles
UK	United Kingdom
UN	United Nations
UNSC	United Nations Security Council
UNMEE	United Nations Mission in Ethiopia and Eritrea
US	United States
USJFCOM	United States Joint Forces Command
WEU	West European Union
WMD	Weapons of Mass Destruction

About the Authors

Jeffrey P. Bialos currently serves as Executive Director of the Transatlantic Security and Industry Program at the Center for Transatlantic Relations, and as a partner in the law firm of Sutherland, Asbill & Brennan. He previously served in a number of senior positions in the Clinton Administration, including most recently as Deputy Under Secretary of Defense for Industrial Affairs.

Hans Binnendijk is the Theodore Roosevelt Chair in National Security Policy and Director of the Center for Technology and National Security Policy. He previously served on the National Security Council as Special Assistant to the President and Senior Director for Defense Policy and Arms Control (1999-2001. From 1994 to 1999, Dr. Binnendijk was Director of the Institute for National Strategic Studies at the National Defense University. Prior to that he was Principal Deputy Director of the State Department's Policy Planning Staff (1993-1994).

Yves Boyer is Deputy Director of the Fondation pour la Recherche Stratégique and Chairman of the Société Française d'Etudes Militaires in Paris. He is also a professor at the Ecole Spéciale Militaire de Saint Cyr and Senior Lecturer at the Ecole Polytechnique.

Brigadier General Manfred Engelhardt is Assistant Chief of Armed Forces Staff V Operations, German Ministry of Defense. Prior to this position he was Commander of the 7th Mechanized Infantry Brigade and Division Chief of the Political-Military Directorate in the German Federal Ministry of Defense.

Daniel S. Hamilton is the Richard von Weizsäcker Professor and Director of the Center for Transatlantic Relations at Johns Hopkins University's Paul H. Nitze School of Advanced International Studies. He also serves as Executive Director of the American Consortium on EU Studies (ACES), the EU Center in Washington, DC. He previously served as Deputy Assistant Secretary of State for European Affairs, with particular responsibility for NATO and transatlantic security issues, and as Associate Director of the Policy Planning Staff.

Andrew James is a Research Fellow at the University of Manchester in the United Kingdom where his research focuses on transatlantic and European defense industrial and technology issues and their strategic and security implications. During 2003, he was external expert and Rapporteur on defense issues to the European Union Research Advisory Board (EURAB), a high-level working group on science and technology policy reporting to European Commissioner for Research Philippe Busquin.

Stuart L. Koehl is a defense analyst serving as a Fellow at the Center for Transatlantic Relations. He focuses his research activities on transatlantic security and industrial issues.

Richard L. Kugler is a Distinguished Research Professor at the Center for Technology and National Security Policy, where he performs analyses. His specialty is U.S. defense strategy, global security affairs, and NATO. He advises senior echelons of the Office of Secretary of Defense, the Joint Staff, and the interagency community.

George Robertson The Right Honourable Lord Robertson of Port Ellen was the 10th Secretary General of NATO and Chairman of the North Atlantic Council from 1999-2003. He was Defense Secretary of the United Kingdom from 1997-1999 and Member of Parliament for Hamilton and Hamilton South from 1978-1999.

Rob de Wijk is director of the Clingendael Centre for Strategic Studies. He is also a professor of international relations at the Royal Military Academy (KMA) in Breda, and professor of strategic studies at Leiden University. He previously served as Head of the Defence Concepts Division of the Netherlands Ministry of Defence.